A MUSLIM PRIMER

BEGINNER'S GUIDE TO ISLAM

The Crescent and Star were symbols of the Byzantine Empire. They were later adopted by Islam when it became a ruling power.

Arabic word for *Allah*

Whatever form a minaret takes, this prominent tower is the place from which the muezzin calls faithful Muslims to prayer.

Illustrated by Jody Kathryn Zepp

A
MUSLIM
PRIMER

BEGINNER'S GUIDE TO ISLAM

Ira G. Zepp, Jr.

Sheed and Ward
London

Copyright © 1992 by Ira G. Zepp, Jr. First published 1992.
ISBN 0 7220 5710 5. All rights reserved. Printed in U.S.A.
for Sheed & Ward Ltd, 2 Creechurch Lane, London EC3A 5AQ.

*For Bill and Joan Edwards—
lifelong and dear friends*

Not to be informed about the world's fastest growing religion may lead us to perpetuate myths that are the fruit of prejudice and not understand the religious experience of those who are already or may soon be our neighbors.

Thomas R. Hurst

It is not righteousness that you turn your faces to the East or the West, but righteous is he who believes in God and the Last Day and the Angels and the Book and the Prophets; and gives his wealth for love of Him to kinsfolk and to orphans and the needy and the wayfarer and to those who ask, and to set slaves free, and observes proper worship and pays the Zakah. And those who keep their treaty when they make one, and the patient in tribulation and adversity and time of stress; such are those who are sincere. Such are the Godfearing.

Quran 2:177

I believe in the fundamental truth of all great religions of the world. I believe that they are all God-given, and I believe that they were necessary for the people to whom these religions were revealed. And I believe that, if only we could all of us read the scriptures of the different faiths from the standpoint of the followers of those faiths, we should find that they were at the bottom all one and were helpful to one another.

Mahatma Gandhi

CONTENTS

ACKNOWLEDGMENTS

Posted in my office are these words from an anonymous sage: "I have drunk from wells I did not dig; I have been warmed by fires I did not build; I have been shaded by trees I did not plant." This general truth about life applies to the preparation of this *Primer*. It is my pleasant task to acknowledge my indebtedness to many people who helped make this book a reality.

Authors usually express appreciation to their families at the end of an acknowledgment section with "and last but by no means least." I wish to thank my wife, Mary, and my daughter, Jody, first and by all means most, for their immeasurable encouragement, support, and patience while this book was being written. I also greatly appreciate their measurable contributions, which include artwork and photography.

I am also grateful to the following:
—The Philosophy and Religious Studies Department and the Faculty Development Committee of Western Maryland College for a grant to study at the Duncan Black Macdonald Center for the Study of Islam and Christian-Muslim Relations at Hartford Seminary in Hartford, Connecticut, in June of 1991.
—Western Maryland College for a sabbatical leave in the Spring of 1991 which allowed me to complete this book.

—The Library staff at Hartford Seminary and to Hartford Seminary faculty members Dr. Wadi Z. Haddad and Dr. Ibrahim Abu-Rabi from whom, respectively, I had courses on the Quran and Islamic thought. I am particularly grateful to Dr. Abu-Rabi for his hermeneutical insights which were invaluable for my research. He, by the way, is the first Muslim to be hired as a full-time faculty member of any seminary affiliated with the American Association of Theological Schools.

—Dr. M. Sayyid M. Syeed of the International Institute of Islamic Thought in Herndon, Virginia, for providing valuable resources for my research and for his generous introduction to this *Primer*.

—M. Bashan Arafat, Imam and Director of the Islamic Society of Baltimore, and its office manager Sister Kim, for their advice and cooperation.

—Muhammad Magid, Librarian of The Islamic Center of Washington, D.C., for education aids.

—Lee Vinzant of the Public Affairs Department of Aramco World in Houston, Texas, who provided several photographs of Islamic architecture.

I wish to thank the following persons with whom I have talked this past year:

—my Muslim students: Can Figan and Marcus Abutorabi at Harlaxton College, England; and Alihan Ciftcioglu, Dina and Nora Soloman at Western Maryland College.

—David Harden, who worked for two years in Pakistan.

—Roma Jo and R. Jan Thompson, who lived for some time in Sudan.

The following friends and colleagues read the manuscript and made valuable suggestions:

—Dr. Melvin Palmer, Professor of Comparative Literature at Western Maryland College.

—Dr. Julie Badiee, Professor of Art History and a specialist in Islamic Art, and her husband, Heshmat Badiee, both of Western Maryland College.

—Dr. Sayyid and Yusuf Talal DeLorenzo of the International Institute of Islamic Thought who spotted inaccuracies about Islam in the text.

—Dorothy Shindle, whose combination of competence, conscientiousness, and creativity is a rare find these days. Dorothy typed the final two drafts, made many helpful suggestions about style, and was indispensable in making the manuscript ready for the publisher. Her efficiency and reliability know no bounds.

—John McHale, publisher of Wakefield Editions, who displayed his customary foresight, guidance, and patience.

While many people have made contributions to various sections of this *Primer,* I assume full responsibility for its contents.

IGZ

PREFACE

I had my first impression of Islamic culture while on a Fulbright Fellowship to India twenty-five years ago. Although my task then was to study Hinduism, a comparative look at Islam and its Indian expression was unavoidable. The architectural beauty and aesthetic legacy of the Mughal empire expressed in the mosques at Fatephur Sikri and in Delhi, especially the Jamma Masjid and the timelessly fascinating Taj Mahal and Red Fort, were unforgettable.

On two different trips to the Middle East—one a summer seminar at the Hebrew University in Jerusalem—I visited the Sultan Ahmad Mosque in Istanbul (popularly known as the Blue Mosque), the famous Al-Azhar, the intellectual heart of the Islamic world in Cairo, as well as the Dome of the Rock and the Al-Aqsa Mosque in Jerusalem. From my hotel and dormitory windows, I heard the *Muadhdhin* (muezzin) call faithful Muslims in these cities to prayer.

While hosting a television documentary on world religions in 1977, I met and interviewed Muhammad Abdul Rauf, then director of the Islamic Center in Washington, D.C. As a token of gratitude he gave me a copy of the widely used translation and commentary of the *Quran* by A. Yusuf Ali. It was a touching and gracious moment. In humility and appreciation, he said, "Please do not place anything on this holy book." I had a real sense of the sacredness of this scripture; to this day the book remains a prized possession. I am thankful for these first-hand experiences of Islam. They have enriched my understanding and teaching of world religions.

Three main factors prompted the writing of this book. First, during the past five years, I have met not only with students in my own religious studies classes, but also with many adult education classes in churches around the Baltimore-Washington area to help them engage in Muslim-Christian dialogue. My wife and I have also conducted several clergy retreats in which interfaith dialogue played a prominent role.

I have learned from hundreds of lay people, especially those at Hiss, Glyndon, and Westminster United Methodist Churches as well as those in the Ascension Episcopal Church, St. Mary's United Church of Christ, the Unitarian-Universalists of Northwest Baltimore, and Westminster Church of the Brethren. In addition, clergy colleagues provided insights to help me focus issues of interfaith dialogue.

Those fellow clergy as well as students and lay people have asked the questions which generated and informed the content of this *Primer*. Here is a list of questions most frequently asked:

> *How did Islam begin?*
> *What are the beliefs of Islam?*
> *Are there any similarities between*
>   *Christianity and Islam?*
> *What do Muslims believe about Christ?*
> *What is their belief about salvation?*
> *Is forgiveness of sin valued?*
> *What are the major symbols and rituals of Islam?*
> *What are Muslim prayer customs?*
> *Is the God of Islam merciful or judgmental?*
> *What is the place of women in Islam?*
> *What is the Muslim attitude toward peace?*

What authority is given to their holy men?
Why is Islam so popular and growing?
How can I simply define Islam?
What are the differences between
  Sunni and Shiite Muslims?

These questions were asked over and over again. It became clear to all of us that there was a need for a beginner's guide to Islam that would not necessarily serve as a college text or act as a resource for the professional scholar.[1]

Another reason for this *Primer,* a kind of "Islam for Every Person," is to help correct distortions, stereotypes, and discrimination relative to Arabs and their culture. We need only recall the media sound bites, catch phrases, and bumper sticker depictions of Islam that we heard and saw prior to, during, and after the recent Persian Gulf War. These abbreviations have inevitably distorted a revered religious tradition and culture almost beyond recognition. They betray the lack of knowledge about Arabs and Islam on the part of the western press, our politicians and religious leaders, and the average American citizen.

The negative press began with the Suez crisis in 1956 and continued through the oil embargo of 1973, the Iranian hostage crisis in 1979, and most recently, the Gulf War. As a result, "Ayatollah," "Shiite Fundamentalism," "resurgent Islam," and "Islamic revolution" became household phrases.

In this context, the Arab has become the new villain in our cartoons, the new scapegoat in our language, another person or group we love to hate and conveniently demonize and stereotype. Yvonne Haddad of the University of Massachusetts, on Bill Moyers' PBS special on the Arabs in the

Spring of 1991, described the evolution of this stereotyping in the twentieth century. "The Arab," she said, "was first a 'camel jockey' (remember Lawrence of Arabia?), then he was an oil tycoon with a stretch limousine; finally, in the last ten years, the Arab has become the terrorist."

What logically follows from this negative imaging is discrimination against Arabs in this country. In a December 21, 1990, edition of *The Los Angeles Times,* former U.S. Senator James Abourezk, who now heads the American-Arab Anti-Discrimination Committee, noted that since the 1973 oil embargo, discrimination against Arabs and other Muslims has substantially increased.

Some examples: A Baltimore neighborhood isolated a Muslim family so effectively that the family decided to move. At China Lake Naval Weapons Center in California, workers wore T-shirts that portrayed U.S. warplanes bombing an Arab riding a camel and inscribed on the shirt was: "I'd fly 7,000 miles to destroy a camel." In Houston, a Saudi Arabian couple was physically assaulted at a shopping mall as the attackers cried: "You're Arabs!"

Bruce Lawrence, professor of History at Duke University, in a brilliant new book, *Defenders of God,* outlines the conversion to Islam of Neil Armstrong, the first astronaut to land on the moon. In the book he tells how Armstrong was warned to keep his new religion to himself or he could be fired from his government job.[2]

There is a long history of anti-Muslim feeling in the West. Dante, however sophisticated he might otherwise have been, was captive to medieval Christian bias. He condemned the "arch heretic" Muhammad, split from head to waist, to the lower circles of hell.

Apart from a course in comparative religion and a passing reference to Averroes in a history of philosophy, hardly a mention of Islam was made during my undergraduate days or even in my theological studies. That, in itself, is an interesting historical issue. Why did we not hear of the tremendous cultural impact of Islam on western culture, the part Islam played in effecting the Protestant Reformation, and the philosophical, literary, and scientific debt we owe Islam? Only in the past decade have universities begun to take Islam seriously as a legitimate academic subject.

A final reason we should be learning about Islam, if only for self-interest, is its sheer numerical mass. There are one billion Muslims in the world, which is about the same number Christianity claims. Both tend to be triumphalist, one-way, proselytizing religions. The twenty-first century will force these two major global religious and cultural forces to engage each other in a far more enlightened way than they have in the past fourteen hundred years.

Furthermore, there are about four to five million Muslims in the United States, making Islam the third largest religion in our country. That is more than Episcopalians or Presbyterians or Lutherans or the United Church of Christ. By the year 2000, Islam will surpass Judaism as our second largest religion. Over one-third of the Muslims in the United States belong to the American Muslim Mission and The Nation of Islam. Islam's appeal to people of color is not lost on many African Americans. This is the force behind the name changes of many African Americans, of Malcolm X to Malik El-Shabazz, of Lew Alcindor to Kareem Abdul-Jabbar, of Cassius Clay to Muhammad Ali, and of Leroi Jones to Imamu Amiri Baraka.

CENTERS OF MUSLIM POPULATION

1.	Indonesia	161 million
2.	Bangladesh	100 million
3.	Nigeria	100 million
4.	Pakistan	90 million
5.	Turkey	60 million
6.	Egypt	51 million
7.	Morocco	24 million
8.	Algeria	22 million
9.	Sudan	22 million
10.	Afghanistan	18 million
11.	Malaysia	14.5 million
12.	Iraq	14.5 million
13.	Syria	11 million
14.	Saudi Arabia	10.5 million
15.	Tunisia	7 million
16.	Senegal	7 million
17.	Somalia	5 million
18.	Chad	4 million
19.	Jordan	3 million
20.	Libya	3 million
21.	Mauritania	2 million
22.	Kuwait	1 million

SOME COUNTRIES WITH MUSLIM MINORITIES

1.	India	100 million
2.	USSR	60 million
3.	China	90 million
4.	France	2 million
5.	United Kingdom	2 million
6.	West Germany	1.5 million

Source: Ministry of Islamic Affairs, Kuwait, 1985

An American Muslim woman working in The
Islamic Center of Baltimore. [Photo by Mary D. Zepp]

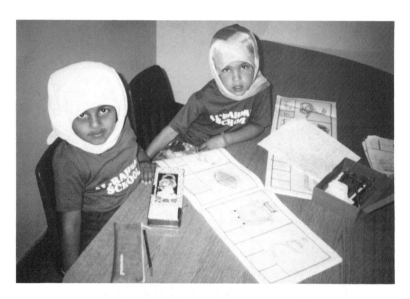

Two Muslim girls in schoolroom.
[Photo courtesy of Islamic Center of Baltimore]

Imam leading Muslim boys in prayer.
[Photo courtesty of Islamic Center of Baltimore]

Increasingly, Muslims are our neighbors, They are found in the cities of New York, Chicago, Washington, Houston, Los Angeles and in their suburbs; they are teaching in our schools and colleges, running businesses, and working in our hospitals and government agencies. Only last June 25, 1991, Siraj Wahaj, the Imam of Masjid al Taqwa in Brooklyn, New York, became the first Muslim to offer the daily prayer for the House of Representatives.

Interior of Mosque at The Islamic Center of Washington, D.C. At left is the *Mihrab* (niche in wall) which is the *Qibla* or direction of Mecca. At right is the *Minbar* (pulpit) from which Friday sermons are preached. [Courtesy: The Islamic Center of Washington, D.C.]

The Islamic Center of Washington, D.C. It contains a mosque and an institute for higher study of Islamic culture. [Courtesy: Islamic Center of Washington, D.C.]

For many years now I have taught college religious studies courses from a comparative standpoint. This method involves comparison of the best in one religion with the best in another, not the best in one religion with the worst in another. You will see in this book that I attempt to discuss the ideal and normative nature of Islam rather than how ineffectively it is practiced by some Muslims or how far others deviate from the norm. I have used primarily Muslim sources rather than what Western orientalists have said about Islam. It is my conviction that Western readers should be presented a broad spectrum of Muslim opinion because Islam is no more monolithic than Christianity. To that end I have referred to the polemical Abdalati *(Islam in Focus)*, the catechetical al-Qaradawi *(The Lawful and the Prohibited in Islam),* the conservative al-Faruqi *(The Cultural Atlas of Islam),* and the progressive F. Rahman *(Major Themes of the Quran).* Furthermore, I have tried to allow the essence of Islam to dictate the data I present, rather than forcing information about Islam into a predetermined mold. This permits me to distinguish Islam from the history of Muslim faith, just as I would want to distinguish Jesus from the history of Christianity.

A Muslim Primer is for the ordinary individual who wants a "taste" of Islam, for the person on the street, the nonprofessional who may never have a chance to take a college course or a six-week seminar in a local church or synagogue. I would hope that anyone interested in a brief, clear overview of Islam could pick up this book and find it informative. It intentionally attempts to distill and broker a vast amount of material for the average reader.

There is a need not only to know about the content of Islam; there is a corollary need to develop skills of encountering another culture and religion in such a way as to elicit the truth of that religion without finding too many of our own thumb prints on it. So I want to speak with the voice of a sympathetic interpreter of Islam, but from time to time I may speak with the detached voice of a historian of religion.

Islam will be presented with no intentional value judgments; it will be treated the way we would like Christianity to be treated—fairly, positively, without bias. I will strive to turn up the light and turn down the heat, to moderate the all too often emotional approaches we Western Christians bring to a discussion of Islam. In this way, we will find that Islam is no more strange than any other religion. For those who are interested, a list of guidelines and suggestions for Muslim-

Christian dialogue will be found in the conclusion of the book.

I have in my mind's eye the picture of Jewish Prime Minister Menachem Begin of Israel, Muslim President Anwar Sadat of Egypt, and the Christian President Jimmy Carter of the United States joining hands at Camp David in 1978. My hope is that someday, sooner rather than later, this symbolic gesture will become a reality—that all of Abraham's children will live in Shalom, Peace, and Salam and that these "People of the Book" will engage in a fruitful "trialogue."

Ira G. Zepp, Jr.
Western Maryland College
Westminster, Maryland
August 1991

INTRODUCTION

I would like to congratulate Professor Ira Zepp for writing this book introducing the basic truths about Islam. The massive journalistic literature that is being produced in the West on Islam is extremely misleading and often appears to be designed to demonize Islam. Muslims are faced every day, right and left, with anti-Islamic books, newspaper articles, radio and television commentaries and news selected to misrepresent and distort the meaning and message of Islam.

The misrepresentation of Islam is a legacy of the Crusades era providing justification for confrontation and colonization of Muslim lands. Dante's dream about the Prophet of Islam was a realization of centuries of false propaganda and vilification of Islam. An enlightening book, *A Muslim Primer: Beginner's Guide to Islam* is soothing and comforting. It is important that scholars with an objective outlook and a concern for building bridges rather than further widening the centuries-old gulf come forward and provide balanced materials on Islam.

It is in the interests of the common good of mankind in general to let Islam be represented objectively in the West in its real spirit. Let it be known that Islam's mission is not the disrespect of other religions, rather an attempt to strengthen the common roots of all faiths. The Qur'an makes it clear that the divine message has been sent through the ages to different nations and different regions around the world. The

Qur'anic verse 35:24 says: "Every nation has had a Warner [a Prophet of God]."

This raises the possibilities that every nation has had the divine revelation at one time or the other. Therefore all religions must have at the core a teaching that needs to be recognized and respected.

There has been continuity of the monotheistic message through the prophets Adam, Noah, Abraham, Moses, and Jesus, and many others who may not have been mentioned by name in the Qur'an.

> We sent messengers before you [Muhammad]—of them are those that We have mentioned to you (by name) and of them are those We have not mentioned to you. (40:78)

The Qur'an declares:

> Say we believe in Allah, and the revelation given to us, and to Abraham, Ishmael, Isaac, Jacob, and the tribes and that given to Moses and Jesus and that given to all prophets from their Lord: We make no difference between one another among them. (2:136)

This is the foundation of the Islamic creed. It inculcates a sense and spirit of cooperation with other religions. Islam gives a special status to the Jews and Christians. They are called the "People of the Book [scriptures]." The Muslims are exhorted by the Qur'an to invite the People of the Book to a common dialogue (3:6). In another reference to the People of the Book, the Qur'an tells Muslims:

> There are people among them who stand by their Covenant, recite the word of Allah in the hours of

night and prostrate before Him. They believe in
Allah, and the last day of judgment, and enjoin what
is good and forbid what is evil, and try to excel each
other in good works. And these are among the virtuous. And whatever good they do, they shall not be
denied its due reward and Allah knows well who are
the God fearing. (3:13)

These teachings lay firm foundations for mutual respect and
recognition of Abrahamic faiths and provide a basis for
meaningful dialogue.

The Qur'an forbids Muslims from fighting against those
who are not oppressors.

Allah forbids you not from dealing kindly and justly
with those who are not fighting against you or driving you out of your homes for Allah loves who are
just.

Allah only forbids you from making friends with
those who are fighting against you on account of
your religion and driving you out of your homes,
and have helped others in driving you out of your
homes, and whoever makes friends with them, these
are the transgressors. (60:9-10)

Islam's emphasis on the unity of human race, equality of all
humans before God is expressed in these verses:

O mankind! We created you from a single [pair] of a
male and a female, and made you into nations and
tribes, that you may recognize each other. Indeed,
the most honorable among you in the sight of Allah
is the most righteous of you. And Allah has full
knowledge and is well aware of all this."

In fact Prophet Muhammad (peace be unto him) described mankind as "a family of Allah, the best of you are the ones who are sources of greatest benefit to other fellow humans."

It is this egalitarian spirit of Islam that has brought together different colors, races, and nations into the Islamic world community. In North America, the Muslim community has been growing through immigration, conversion, and births. Islamic organizations and Islamic centers have emerged from coast to coast in the U.S. Many Christians and Jews visit Muslim places of worship and watch Muslims pray and perform their religious rites. There are regular dialogues and trialogues sponsored by the followers of the three religions. We believe that this kind of healthy interaction between believers is going to ensure an era of understanding, mutual enrichment, and peace and prosperity to the human race.

We hope Professor Ira Zepp's book will provide a breakthrough in terms of furthering an objective appreciation of the Islamic faith in the U.S. and elsewhere. We pray to Allah to provide all believers right vision, right understanding, and the right spirit to lead mankind out of the present misery, suffering and confusion.

Sayyid Muhammad Syeed, Ph.D.
General Secretary
The Association of Muslim Social Scientists
International Institute of Islamic Thought
Herndon, Virginia

FOREWORD
Historical Context
for Contemporary Interest in Islam

"We are not terrorists; we don't hijack airplanes."

That was the response of three Muslim students when I asked them "What would you like westerners to know about Islam?" (May 1991)

For several centuries before the 1979 takeover of the American Embassy by Islamic students in Teheran and the subsequent captivity of American hostages for 444 days, most westerners had not taken Islam very seriously. A minority of western people champion the cause of Palestine refugees and try to understand the painful history which at the same time divides and unites Jews and Arabs. But on political and emotional balance, the majority of Americans and Europeans sympathize with Israel. This has prevented us from feeling the tremors from the Islamic world, from hearing the voice of the Muslim soul, and from appreciating the human experience of one-fifth of the world's population.

A brief historical perspective is in order to help us understand why we have ignored such a rich and vibrant culture, why we in the West have had continuing strife with Islamic countries, and especially why we are confused about what is called the "roots of Muslim rage."

Let us recall that for about a thousand years after Muhammad's death, Muslims were on the march through the Middle East, North Africa, and Europe. In that process Muslims almost won the known world for Islam. This new religiopolitical force was finally stopped by threatened and strongly mobilized European armies. At the same time, while Europe was in the so-called Dark Ages, Islam was creating an advanced and sophisticated culture in such places as Baghdad, Cairo, and Cordova. This period was known as Islam's "Golden Age" or the "Classical Period." No field of human endeavor was untouched by Muslim genius. Discoveries, explorations, and insights in Mathematics, Medicine, Astronomy, Philosophy, Literature, and Science all happened during this period. Many of them were eventually shared with the West. A later chapter will detail some of the gifts of Islam to world culture.

Then in the fifteenth century, the Ottoman Empire conquered Constantinople (now Istanbul) and that empire controlled most of the Middle East until well into the first quarter of the twentieth century. The European response to the Ottoman hegemony, which also began in the sixteenth century, was to colonize as much of the rest of the world as possible, including the Americas, Africa, and a good deal of Asia. This empire building lasted for about 400 years.

After World War I, and the demise of the Ottoman Empire, the League of Nations assigned most of the Middle East to France and Great Britain. Iraq, Jordan (then Trans-Jordan), Palestine, and some Gulf states went to Britain. Syria and Lebanon went to France. Through it all, Saudi Arabia remained independent. But by 1920, most of the Muslim world was under some form of colonial rule by a western power.

The United States never colonized the Middle East in a military or politically imperial way. However, our need for oil, discovered there in the first decade of this century, allied us with and sometimes forced us to support leaders such as the Shah of Iran, who did not represent what traditional Islam holds dear.

It was a classic clash of cultural values. Many Muslims called it "Westoxification" and many Americans thought Muslims "undeveloped." We could not or did not desire to share the basic values of Islam. A sizeable number of Muslims, Sunni and Shiite alike, see the materialism and technocratic mind-set of the West (itself a stereotype) as barriers to their worship of Allah and a threat to the very foundation of Islamic family life and the larger Muslim society. So they felt put upon and violated by us, and to a degree, they saw themselves colonized by the economic power of western countries, the United States in particular.

World War II saw the emergence of two super powers, the United States and the Soviet Union. At the same time, western European countries saw a weakening of their hold on the colonies in Asia and Africa. Now that the colonial powers have withdrawn from the Middle East, Muslim nations are again drawing attention to themselves and are a force to be dealt with in international politics.

Much of this attention is fueled by anger, a sense of humiliation, and a loss of self-esteem. Bernard Lewis, well-known orientalist who taught at the University of London and most recently at Princeton University, says that Muslim rage against the West is:

> a growing awareness among the heirs of an old, proud, and long-dominant civilization of having been

overtaken, overborn, and overwhelmed by those whom they had long regarded their inferiors.[3]

This rage has not only triggered tension between the West and Islam; it has also caused conflict among the Middle Eastern neighbors themselves, the likes of which we have not seen for centuries. The kind of inter-tribal warfare going on today between Iraq and Iran, Lebanon and Syria, and Israel and Jordan, are reminiscent of the numerous wars, often religiously motivated, among European nations in the seventeenth and eighteenth centuries.

History is a reliable teacher, and the understanding of ourselves and others is deepened if we listen to its message. The message from Islam is that to deny the importance of religion in one's history and identity is to destroy one's culture and one's self.

BY WAY OF DEFINITION

ISLAM   It is pronounced with the accent on the second syllable: *i-SLAM*. The word literally means submission, obedience, or surrender. Islam, however, is derived from *Salam*, the Arabic word for peace. So a literal definition of Islam is "peace through submission to the will of Allah."

Islam is the name of the religion. The religion is not, as with Christianity, Buddhism, and other religions, named after its founder. It is wrong to call Islam "Muhammadanism"; as Huston Smith says, it would be like calling Christianity "St. Paulism." Muslims believe God, not Muhammad, founded their religion. Muhammad played a crucial role in the formulation of Islam, but he is secondary to Allah and the Quran in terms of importance and status. Muhammad is not divine nor an incarnation of God, nor is he worshiped in any way.

MUSLIM   The person who practices Islam is a Muslim or Muslima, that is, a surrendered one, one who has submitted to God. You become a Muslim, not by birth, but by confession of the *Shahadah,* "There is no God but one God and Muhammad is the Prophet of God," and by practicing the good deeds prescribed by the Quran. Islam's appeal is its simplicity; it is not "Simple-Simon simple," but it is uncomplicated, straightforward, and easy to understand. Entrance into Islam is not conditioned by a religious experience, the reception of sacraments, or belief in theological fine points. A Muslim is a person who can make the twin declaration of the Shahadah and a righteous life.

Hence, Islam is less of a religion, as many contemporary westerners usually understand the word, and more of a total way of life. Politics, art, education, daily routine, diet, and many social customs are guided by Allah and are infused with the spirit of Islam. Because of this, Islam is not easily reduced to cultural forms, social systems, or psychological states. It is a way of life, confidently embracing this world, and a preparation for the after-life, just as confidently embracing the other world.

Beyond the simplicity of the Islamic core, that is, the Shahadah and the Five Pillars of faith, there is as much heterogeneity in Islam as you find in any religion. Its diversity is found from country to country, from America to Algeria to Arabia, from India to Indonesia. There are modernist and traditionalist Muslims, liberal and conservative ones, sincere and insincere, and devout and lax Muslims.

You can see a similar diversity in Christianity. There are many Christian expressions—from the ecstasy of snake-handling Pentecostals in West Virginia to the sedate Presbyterian liturgy in New Jersey to the sensual Catholic Mass in New England. Jerry Falwell and Bishop James Spong are Protestant Christians. Daniel Berrigan and Cardinal Ratzinger are Catholic Christians. Adolf Hitler and Martin Luther King, Jr., were both Christians. There are "Sunday Christians" and daily devout Christians. Anwar Sadat was, and Saddam Hussein is, a Sunni Muslim; Al-Ghazali, brilliant twelfth-century Sufi, and Ayatollah Khomenei, a brilliant Shiite theologian, were both faithful Muslims. We don't want to stereotype a religion by looking at one person or one event in its history. A sign of spiritual and intellectual maturity is the courage to accept diversity within and between religions and cultures.

I have taken the lead of long-time Islamic scholar Kenneth Cragg and, for the most part, will use Islam as the ideal and definitive reference for the religion, and Muslim to express the actual, empirical, and particular expression of the faith.

ARAB The word literally means "nomad," but for our purposes, an Arab is someone who speaks Arabic and shares a common history with other Arabs, just as a German is one who shares a common language and cultural heritage. Westerners tend to identify Islam with Arabs. True, the religion started in Arabia and Muhammad was an Arab, the greatest Arab who ever lived. But, Iran, one of the most Muslim of countries, has a separate language and different ethnic background from the Arabs. So, whereas 90% of Arabs are Muslims, only 20% of Muslims are Arab. Egypt is the largest Arab country with a population of 48 million, while Indonesia is the largest Muslim country with 161 million followers. This is not to mention that there are several million Arab Jews and Christians, who also call God Allah and could have "Muslim" names like Abdullah (servant of God).

Some additional notes for the reader:

1. I have avoided the use of diacritical marks in the English versions of Arabic words to make the text more readable for the introductory student.

2. I have used "God" and "Allah" interchangeably because the Quran understands these two words to refer to the same divine reality.

3. Islamic theologians and the Quran are at home with gender exclusive language for God and so to maintain the integrity of a participant observer and to be fair to Islam, I have generally adhered to Muslim usage.

4. The translation of the Quran I have used most is Abdullah Yusuf Ali's, although, from time to time, I have consulted other translations. The numbering of the verses, however, is exclusively Yusuf Ali's.

Part One
The Desert is Fertile

Abraham:
First Monotheist and Common Parent

A profound right-angle turn was made in the history of religion during the nineteenth century BCE. A man named Abraham (Ibrahim in Arabic) dared to challenge his father's authority and reject his household gods. He did so in the name of a new God he had experienced. It is important here to recognize that Adam was the first in the line of prophets (3:33) and although Islam was renewed by Noah, in Abraham's time there was much corruption of the monotheism God intended in creation. The Quran puts it this way: "Tell of Abraham, who said to Azur, his father, 'Will you worship idols as your gods? Surely you and all your people are in palpable error.' " (6:74-84) The Biblical version of the story is found in Genesis 12.

Abraham's father, Terah (Azur was his Arabic name), took his family from the Chaldean city of Ur in the Mesopotamian Valley to Haran on the northwest arc of the fertile crescent. From Haran, Abraham followed the beckoning of his new God to Canaan, Egypt, and back to Canaan, the land his God had promised him. Islam believes this journey also took Abraham to Mecca. This same spiritual and geographical pilgrimage by the world's first monotheist and first Hanif spawned three major religions: Judaism, Christianity, and Islam. Each of them confesses Abraham to be the "friend of

God and father of the faithful" and for each of them, the history of salvation began with Abraham and his covenant with God.

Judaism, Christianity, and Islam each has a special claim on Abraham. Jews believe he was the original covenant maker with God, establishing circumcision as the sign of that special relationship. So Abraham was a Jew before the Torah. St. Paul, in the Christian tradition, saw Abraham's unconditional faith in God as a model of Christian justification by grace, and so Abraham was a Christian before the Gospel. For Muslims, Abraham's willingness to sacrifice his son is the prototype of submission (Islam), and so he was a Muslim before the Quran.

How this shared heritage played itself out in history is interpreted differently by the three faith communities. Our general concern here is that Abraham is the tribal ancestor of Israel and Arab people by way of two women, Hagar and Sarah, and two sons, Ishmael and Isaac.

Since Abraham is more important to Islam than to the other major western religions, our specific emphasis is Islam's view of Abraham and his place in its tradition. For all intents and purposes, Islam got off the ground with Abraham, but during the succeeding centuries it was distorted and altered. The mission of Muhammad was to restore Islam to its pristine purity.

As we review the story of Abraham, we will see how similar and how different the Hebrew and Islamic versions are. God made a covenant with Abraham and promised him that his family and its descendants would be many and blessed. Sarah, Abraham's wife, did not believe God could fulfill the promise since she was well past child-bearing age. So she took matters into her own hands and encouraged Abraham to take another wife, her Egyptian maid, Hagar.

Abraham and Hagar had a son who was named Ishmael, that is, "God hears" or "The Lord had given heed"—presumably to Sarah's incapacity to have children. Soon after Ishmael was circumcised at age thirteen, a second son was miraculously born to Sarah. This son was Isaac, who figures prominently in the Hebrew story. Because Sarah feared, perhaps out of jealousy, that Ishmael, the first-born and legitimate heir to God's promise, might compete with Isaac for this heritage, she, with Abraham's consent, forced Hagar and Ishmael out of the household. They were banished to fend for themselves in the wilderness.

However, God continued to look out for them. After traveling for days in the scorching desert, Ishmael and Hagar were provided water by God near where the first Kaaba would be built by Abraham. Eventually, as she had hoped, Hagar saw her son marry an Egyptian woman. From that marriage came twelve sons (called "princes" in Genesis 25). Many years later Ishmael and Isaac were reunified as they returned to bury their father. Ishmael, we are told, lived 137 years. Both Judaism and Islam agree with the story thus far.

Of particular importance to Islam is that God had an intimate relation with Abraham and Ishmael and promised to make a great nation from Ishmael's offspring (Genesis 2:13-18). Islam claims that the great nation promised to Ishmael is the Arab people who eventually produced the Prophet Muhammad. This is a crucial difference in interpretation as we shall soon see.

Islam further claims that the wilderness of Paran to which Hagar and Ishmael were banished was the desert area around Mecca. Abraham either went to Paran with them or joined them there, for Muslim tradition states that Abraham and Ishmael built the first Kaaba as a house of worship for Allah (Sura 2:127). It was in Mecca that Hagar discovered the well which mysteriously appeared to assuage Ishmael's thirst. The well is called Zamzam and stands today near the Kaaba. Visiting the well is an integral part of the Muslim's pilgrimage to Mecca.

The indispensability of Ishmael to the Islamic story is seen in its interpretation of Abraham's willingness to sacrifice a son to God. Islam believes the son who was to have been sacrificed was Ishmael, not Isaac. Here is the reasoning.

Ishmael was the firstborn and legally could claim the family birthright. Since Islam makes no distinction between slaves (Hagar) and free people (Sarah), the birthright could not be taken from Ishmael. He was every bit as legitimate a son as his younger brother, Isaac. The Egyptian Islamic scholar, Hammudah Abdalati, represents the best in Muslim faith as he reflects on the discrimination against Hagar: "The status of one's ancestors, the nobility or humbleness of the mother, and the social origin or color shades have no bearing on the spiritual and human quality of man, at least not in the sight of God."[4]

Furthermore, the covenant between God and Abraham, and by implication Ishmael, was made before Isaac was born. So, Ishmael is the "child of promise," the rightful heir to Abraham's patrimony. It is Islam's position that in the Genesis account Isaac's name was substituted for Ishmael's to reinforce the Hebrew role in salvation history. The upshot of all this is that Islam believes that when God ordered Abraham "to take thy son, thine only son...for the burnt offering," God was referring to Ishmael, the firstborn, circumcised, legitimate son of the covenant. (See Sura 37:100-106 for the Quranic account of the story.) Islam sees the Torah's exclusion of Ishmael from the story in the name of the Jewish and later Christian chosen-ness as a way of excluding Arabs and Muslims from the plan of God.

This is in no way to denigrate Isaac, who is one of the Prophets for whom Islam has the highest regard. It is to see how the rights of firstborn sons were perceived in ancient desert culture. The history of the Middle East has been forever shaped by this interpretation of Abraham's covenant and submission to God. On this point hangs a 4000-year-old fratricidal struggle between Israel and Islam. It also explains why Jews could not accept Muhammad as the Messiah.

However divisive the past has been for them, Jews, Christians, and Muslims remain united at the level of a common parent, Abraham. Perhaps the Quran says it best: "Abraham was not a Jew nor yet a Christian; But he was true in faith and bowed his will to God's, and he joined no gods with God." (3:67, see also 2:135-136) Islamic logic concludes that all true followers of Abraham, Moses, and Jesus are Muslims.

From Animism to Allah: Pre–Islamic Arabia

Geography as Latent History

It was certainly true of pre–Islamic Arabia that geography determined history. Roughly the size of the United States east of the Mississippi with Texas thrown in, Arabia was for years a bridge between East and West, Asia and Africa, India and Egypt.

We often forget that Arabia is a peninsula, surrounded on the west by the Red Sea, on the east by the Persian Gulf, and on its southern shore by the Arabian Sea. The northern boundary of Arabia was desert, and just north of that was the famous Fertile Crescent—an arc of oases and productive land stretching from Egypt to the Tigris and Euphrates rivers.

Camel caravans, trade routes, and international travel were commonplace in this "bridge land," especially among those who lived in south central Arabia. Traders with packed camels, bringing incense, spice, silk, ivory, perfume, precious stones, and other exotic goods, passed through Arabia.

These traders brought with them, as well, different ideas and customs. It was no accident then that Arabia became a mixture of races and ethnicity—a cross-cultural community which reflected Persian, Semitic, and African influences, and the social customs of indigenous Arabian tribes.

It seems the Arabs had the capacity to adjust to and assimilate the social patterns and values brought to them from international travelers. This gave southern Arabia and its western coast a relatively sophisticated and cosmopolitan flavor. Excavations in this area have uncovered hints of temples and other public buildings which reflect influences from Persia and Greece. On the other hand, northern Arabia was isolated and parochial.

Pre–Islamic Arabia was organized effectively along tribal lines. These primary human groups were tightly knit and provided needed protection for individuals within the tribe. Tribal solidarity meant security for the whole tribe when it was threatened by rival communities.

Out of economic necessity, tribes would regularly raid each other. Once a tribe was attacked, members were obligated by a rule of honor to avenge the attack. And, conversely, when one person was violated, the entire tribe was wounded and would come to the defense of the hurting individual. The naturalness of this human response was the precursor of blood revenge, eye-for-an-eye ethics, and the justification of defensive war. Primary allegiance to the tribe was the test of one's character and trustworthiness. Betrayal of tribal honor and patriotism was tantamount to treason in Bedouin etiquette. Without the tribe one had neither hope nor safety.

While there may have been hierarchical structures in the tribe, especially along gender lines, there was a remarkable degree of egalitarianism. Some scholars claim that much of tribal life was democratic—people bound together in rights, duties, and responsibilities. The internal cohesion of Islamic society, loyalty to the community and disdain for social rank and class, has its roots in the desert.

Camels were indispensable to nomadic life. They were to the Bedouin what the buffalo was to the Native American. They provided material for tents and clothes, milk and meat for food, and, very importantly, they were beasts of burden which walked the desert dunes with ease. Therefore, soon after their introduction into Arabia about 2000 BCE, camels became a way of measuring wealth. They were the economic base of a country dependent on trade and cross-country travel. Muhammad's ancestral tribe, the Qurasyh, was a prosperous and politically significant group of families in Mecca and was known, among other things, for their activity in the caravan trade. Indeed, Muhammad's first job was helping with camel caravans.

It takes a strong and resilient person to withstand the rigors of desert life. The most courageous and brave are naturally selected to survive this environment of austerity. So certain traits are generated in the harshness of the desert. Sydney Fisher calls them the "manly virtues: bravery in battle, patience in misfortune, protection of the weak, persistence in revenge, and defiance of the strong."[5] Other traits bred by the desert are generosity, hospitality, independence, devotion, and self-sacrifice. It is fascinating to observe how Muhammad embodied many of these personal characteristics in his multifaceted role as warrior, statesman, and religious leader.

Women cared for the family and life in and around the tent. They were especially given the task of guarding the precious commodity of water. Even though they had a strategic part to play in the everyday life of the family, they were often marginalized in terms of the social and political mainstream of the tribe. This exclusion and what appears to us as devaluation of women was seriously addressed by the Quran (see Part Three).

There were no rivers in the Arabian desert. There may have been wadis, dry river beds, which were without water until a rare rainfall came. As a result, oases were a life or death matter, and were invested with divinity and sacred power.

Mecca, a busy cosmopolitan and financial center, was built around a permanent oasis. The economy was reinforced by the flourishing civilization of Yemen to its south and a vibrant agricultural industry in the adjacent countryside. And always there was the spice trade which guaranteed bartering and conversation between peoples representing different ways of life.

But Mecca was not only the hub of a small financial empire. It was also a religious center to which numerous pilgrims from neighboring tribes came regularly to pay homage to their respective deities and to the "small black stone," all of which were housed in the Kaaba. So, by the time of Muhammad, Mecca was a financially sound urban community. In spite of the economically depressed nature of most of Arabia, Mecca benefited from being the crossroads of two kinds of caravans—a commercial one led by camels and a religious one led by devout pilgrims.

Mecca was a center with a centrifugal force, sending traders on their way north to Damascus and Constantinople, and it also experienced a powerful centripetal energy from the faithful, who were attracted to the religious shrine.

Muhammad was born and reared in this Mecca, an exciting crossroads of daily commerce and foreign caravans. As he grew up, he was bound to feel the impact of the ambience of Mecca's bazaars, its pilgrimage sanctuary, and its colorful patrons.

Muhammad also came to know the tension between the Bedouin desert dweller and urban inhabitants of his hometown. To a great extent, Mecca was a socially stratified and class-conscious community. Tension between classes was a direct by-product of an important social and economic change which happened in sixth-century Mecca and throughout the entire Arabian peninsula.

Loyalty to clan, which provided social unity, protection, and welfare for society's helpless, especially widows and orphans, was now severely strained. Reliance upon clan support by needy persons shifted to smaller family units and to business and trading organizations. Muhammad grew up in the midst of this social upheaval. In fact, the very transition Meccan society was undergoing within its borders was evident in how the orphan Muhammad was passed from person to person and family to family. His own life, as we will see later, reflected the changing nature of the larger society.

Religion in Pre–Islamic Arabia
"A Time of Ignorance"

Some scholars, when discussing pre–Islamic Arabian religion, have drawn a distinction between the relatively sedentary life of the farmer and the nomadic life of the desert-dwelling Bedouin. It is finally unresourceful to do this because many religious practices overlapped between these two social groups.

Much of what we know about the myths, symbols, and rituals of the time is found in the condemnation of them by the Quran. This should not surprise us since the Quran was concerned to eliminate the religious heresies which preceded it, namely, the existence of many gods, the fetishes and ritual behavior prevalent in the Hijaz, the area of Arabia in which Mecca and Medina were located.

A "time of ignorance" (*Jahiliyyah*) is what the Quran calls the time in Arabia before the advent of Islam. Pagan cults, polytheism, and a distorted Judaism and Christianity represent an era against which Muhammad reacted with singular passion.

One form of religious expression that particularly bothered Muhammad was what is called animism. The term is somewhat suspect in scholarly circles these days, but for our purposes it simply means that all aspects of nature are invested with sacred powers, that everything is animated, full of life, or inhabited with spiritual forces.

For instance, there was the veneration of stones. Their permanence and durability made them a source of protection from storms and animals, and their coolness and shade supplied an escape from the burning desert sun. The same could be said of trees and glades. The life-giving and sustaining power of water gave springs, wells, and oases a sacred power, often making them places of worship.

Undoubtedly, the devotee saw beyond the stones, trees, and water to the spiritual power in and outside them. At its best, animism did not focus solely on the stones or other aspects of nature which appeared to be worshiped. They were signs pointing to another reality—the spiritual dimension of the universe.

This is particularly true of the Black Stone* in the Kaaba. Legend has it that the Stone was a meteorite which had fallen from heaven centuries before and had been placed in the corner of the Kaaba as a foundation stone by Abraham.

---

*There is a hadith in which the Prophet addresses the black stone, saying that it is no more sacred than the blood and honor of a single Muslim.

Although Muslims retained the age-old practice of touching and kissing it as an integral part of the pilgrimage to Mecca, Muslims attach no sacrality or divinity to it whatsoever.

The second Caliph, Omar, was obviously anxious about the Black Stone being an object of devotion and wanted to extract it from the Kaaba wall altogether. As a relic of Abraham and Ishmael's activity, recognizing the stone in some form was encouraged, but the stone was never worshiped.

Furthermore, Muhammad often used water as an analogy for prayer. "Prayer," he is reported to have said in the Hadith, "is like a stream of sweet water that flows past the door of each of you; into it he plunges five times a day." Finally, the crescent moon and star, both found in nature, are symbols of Islam. But whatever the positive interpretation of animism, Muhammad considered it idolatrous and heathen, clearly illustrating this "time of ignorance."

There was also a profound belief in jinn, who were good and bad spirits found in desolate, fearful places and in places of abundance and fertility. These demonic spirits were propitiated to avoid curses and disaster, and the benevolent spirits were praised to ensure the granting of blessing. In some cases, the good jinn were islamicized into angels, which became a significant part of Muslim faith.

In short, Muhammad was embarrassed by the ancestor cults found among the tribes, the acknowledgment of mountain divinities and astral deities, and the inclination of Arabians to personify natural forces in the oases as god-like figures. In fact, he deplored the whole galaxy of gods available to the farmer, the Bedouin, the merchant, and the town folk. He condemned them as pagan, heathen, and idolatrous—all examples of "ignorance."

In addition to nature worship and polytheism, organized religions had existed for centuries in Arabia before Muhammad. Alongside the pagan religion were small communities of Jews, Christians, and Zoroastrians, especially in western and southern Arabia.

Jewish businessmen were active in the Hijaz and actually dominated commercial life in Yathrib, the original name of Medina. By Muhammad's time, one-half of Medina's population was Jewish and the Jews had accumulated a sizeable amount of land in the nearby oases. Jews also controlled the main bazaar in Medina and much of the city's mercantile interests.

By virtue of St. Paul's trip to Damascus, Christianity had connections with Syria, an area just north of Arabia. From there Christianity's missionary work extended as far south as Mecca. Even though the Christian community in Mecca was small, its presence was visible in the Kaaba. Pictures of Jesus and the Virgin Mary were affixed to its walls. The presence of Judaism and Christianity gave Muhammad an intimate acquaintance with the Torah and the Gospel, the main tenets of each tradition, and an appreciation of them as part of the family of Allah.

Zoroastrianism, a Persian religion which preceded Islam by a millennium, was practiced in Arabia. Along with Judaism and Christianity, Zoroastrianism was a monotheistic religion with Ahura Mazda, the Creator and Wise Lord of this Persian faith, its supreme deity. He was also the father of two spirits, one benevolent and the other evil, similar to the jinn of the Arabian desert. An additionally appealing notion of Zoroastrianism was its insistence on no pictorial replications of God. Muhammad could not help being influenced by all these monotheistic religions.

In fairness, we must say that Allah was not a fulfillment of a pagan religion; He was not the end product of an evolutionary process which began with nature worship, passed through a more discrete polytheism, and finally concluded as the monotheistic deity.

What we can say is that devotion to Allah existed alongside nature gods and goddesses, and in conjunction with astral deities and ancestral worship. Indeed, Islamic tradition traces allegiance to Allah from the time of Abraham and Ishmael's visit to Mecca and their construction of the first Kaaba. As a result, Abraham's god, Allah, was indelibly enshrined in the Arabian pantheon.

The Quran gives us the names of many deities in pre–Islamic Arabia. There were at least five prominent gods—Wadd, Su'ah, Yaqhuth, Ya'uq, and Nasr (see Sura 71:23) and three well-known goddesses—Lat, Manet, and al-Uzza (Sura 53:23). The female divinities represented the Sun, Fortune, and Venus, respectively. They were known as the daughters of Allah and were worshiped by the Qurasyh in Mecca. Some goddess worshipers distilled the feminine deities into one al-Lat who became a partner of Allah, making them a primordial pair which helped with fertility, crops, and oases.

In the midst of the multiplicity of gods and the prevalence of polydemonism were the Hanif, the pure ones, who sought to solidify this menagerie of deities into one singular divinity. The Hanif represented a tradition independent of Judaism and Christianity, but reflected the monotheism of which Abraham's God was the prototype. In retrospect, Muhammad would claim that Islam was not so much the product of an evolutionary process, but a return to Allah's original intention for the world given to his Prophet Abraham, the first Hanif.

So Allah was worshiped before Muhammad, but as a high god, a primary god, a god among other gods. Pre–Islamic Arabia was fertile soil for the affirmation of a single, all-powerful creator God. The religions of Judaism, Christianity, and Zoroastrianism and the work of the native Hanif prepared the way for the Quran's uncompromising monotheism. Muhammad knew his audience had heard of Allah and that he would not have to make a strong case for His existence. His listeners, who might initially resist his message, would not hear his call for one God in a religious vacuum.

Muhammad's assertion that Allah was *the* God was so forceful that all of the remnants of the "time of ignorance" were completely eliminated. Allah was the God of history and nature; no longer was Allah one of the gods, marginalized in the mind of the Bedouin, farmer, and urban dweller. He was now front and center, the Creator of the world, the one, undisputed God. Islam had now come full circle—from Abraham to Muhammad.

Can Anything Good Come Out of Mecca?
The Life of Muhammad

Also, they say, "Why is not this Quran sent down to some leading man in either of the two chief cities?" (43:31)

Muhammad was the Orient's answer to the challenge of Alexander the Great. (Christopher Dawson)

We know very little about Muhammad's life prior to his marriage. The first biography of the Prophet did not appear until a hundred years after his death. But as with all religious founders, there have been attempts to see him as larger than life, to attribute miracles to him, and to see him as an example and model of how one should live. However true it is that members of a religious movement seldom rise higher than the spiritual and ethical standards set by the founder, Muhammad tried desperately to dissuade his followers from adulation and mythicizing his life and work.

The following shall give a brief historical account of Muhammad's life. His religious significance will be discussed at some length in the next section.

> *Did He not find you an orphan and give you shelter?*
> *Did He not find you in error and guide you?*
> *Did He not find you poor and enrich you?*
> *Therefore, do not wrong the orphan, nor chide away the*
> *beggar. But proclaim the goodness of the Lord.*

(93:6-11)

Muhammad's Youth

One of history's auspicious moments occurred about 570 CE in the Arabian oasis town and commercial center of Mecca. To a young couple of the Qurasyh tribe and Banu Hashim clan was born Muhammad ibn Abdullah. He was born on the twelfth day of the third lunar month of Islam's calendar.*

His family was not well-to-do, but they had a fine reputation with a background of nobility and community leadership. They, along with other members of the tribe, were custodians of the sacred Kaaba at the heart of the city. This meant that they were the chief beneficiaries of business brought to Mecca by traders, tourists, and pilgrims. His extended family, the Hashim clan, were first cousins to the Umayads, who were among the Meccan elite and the business and intellectual leaders of the city.

---

*A lunar year consists of six months of twenty-nine days and six months of thirty days—354 days in a year. In every thirty years, there are eleven leap years of 355 days each. So there is a discrepancy of three years in every century of the western calendar. 1991 is the year 1412 of the Islamic calendar.

It is important to note here that Muhammad was not a nomad, but an urban dweller. In fact, many have called Islam's
foundation "the tale of two cities"—Mecca and Medina.
From its beginning, Islam was an urban religion with a
propensity to establish cities, this notwithstanding the fact
that today most Muslims are poor and live in rural areas.

This Arab boy, whose name meant "the highly praised one,"
would grow up to have an impact on the world out of all
proportion to the wealth and status of his family. Not much
was expected from this orphan whose father died two
months before his birth and whose mother died when he was
six. He became a foster child under the care of his grand-
father for a short time and after the latter's death, Muhammad was adopted by an uncle, Abu-Talib.

Even though he was nurtured and protected by this extended
family, one wonders if this early instability helped create his
enthusiastic response to the authoritative and stabilizing message he was later to receive from the angel Gabriel. It surely
is the historical basis for his ethical concern and compassion
for the poor, the orphan, the widows, and other helpless
victims.

The world which his tribal community opened up to him was
a colorful and exciting one of camels, caravans, and the
commerce which accompanied them. Mecca provided scenes
of barter, visits to the shrine of the Black Stone in the
Kaaba, the imaginative language of soothsayers and poets,
and the sale of statues and religious mementos.

By his early teens, Muhammad was traveling with his uncle's caravans to northern Arabia and Syria. He learned fast and well on these business trips with his uncle and the fellow workers. These lessons were the fetal heartbeat of his later business acumen, diplomatic skills, and ability as a statesman. He was so earnest, dependable, and sincere that they nicknamed him al-Amin, "the one who can be trusted."

A graphic description of Muhammad's physical characteristics as he reached his twenties can be found in Muhammad Husayn Haykal's extraordinary biography, *The Life of Muhammad:*

> [He] was handsome of face and of medium build, and neither conspicuously tall nor conspicuously short. He had a large head, very black thick hair, wide forehead, heavy eyebrows, and large black eyes with a light redness on their sides and long eyelashes to add to their attractiveness. He had a fine nose, well spaced teeth, a thick beard, a long handsome neck, wide chest and shoulders, light colored skin, and thick palms and feet. He walked resolutely with firm steps. His appearance was always one of deep thought and contemplation. In his eyes there lurked the authority of a commander of men.[6]

His reputation, reliable character, and good name increased as he matured physically into manhood. This reputation soon reached a wealthy widow and local business woman by the name of Khadija. She hired him to work with her trading company and eventually to supervise her commercial enterprise. So successful was his management of her financial affairs and so responsible was his leadership, that her company prospered beyond expectations.

In time, the business and professional relationship between Muhammad and Khadija shifted to a more personal one. Although she had been married before, had several children, and was fifteen years his senior (Muhammad was twenty-five at the time), she asked him to marry her.

From all we know, they got along well together and their marriage was a happy and compatible one. They had six children, two boys who died in infancy, and four girls. Of the four daughters, only Fatima, the youngest, survived the father. These deaths and bereavements are another example of how Muhammad was acquainted with the brokenness and fragility of life. They deepened his spiritual sensibilities and helped him appreciate the mercy and compassion of Allah.

RECITE!

By the time he was in his thirties, like many a religious reformer before him, Muhammad began a mid-career quest for life's meaning. While he was always a man of modest tastes, he sensed that material welfare was not giving him the personal satisfaction he desired. He began regularly to frequent nearby Mt. Hira for retreat, solitude, and contemplation. As his spiritual search intensified, he became increasingly restless.

Visions, dreams, and trances were all part of this desert experience. "Am I mad?" "Am I fabricating these voices?"
Muhammad asked himself. It seems that he shared the sensitivity of those religious geniuses who walked that fine line
between divine madness, self-doubt, and spiritual creativity.

His most traumatic moment came at age forty around the
27th of the month of Ramadan when he was meditating in a
cave on Mt. Hira. He called it the "Night of Power—better
than a 1000 months...peace until the rising of the dawn."
(97:3,5) A voice as clear and distinct as if it were a friend
next to him said, "Recite in the name of thy Lord and Cherisher who created man of a clot of congealed blood! Proclaim!" (96:1-2)

Muhammad was overwhelmed. "I can't read or write. How
can I do what you command?" was his natural response. He
soon realized that the person speaking to him with such clarity was none other than the angel Gabriel—the same Gabriel
who spoke to Moses and the Virgin Mary. This realization
caused Muhammad greater anxiety. He very quickly shared
the whole experience with Khadija whose opinion he had
long trusted. It is important to say here that, unlike other
founders of religions, such as Jesus and Buddha, Muhammad felt it perfectly natural to be a husband and father with
all the duties required of parenting. In this regard, he returned to the example of Moses and Abraham and other Hebrew messengers of God, for whom it would have been
unthinkable not to be married.

Khadija immediately went to her uncle, a Christian priest, perhaps the only one in Mecca. After she related to him the words Muhammad had received, the uncle replied in effect: "That message we have heard before; it is from God. He is our spiritual brother."

Khadija then assured Muhammad it was an authentic divine revelation; he was not a madman or just another soothsayer. That she was so immediately affirming of Muhammad's vision, that she believed him, trusted him, and defended him against attempts to discredit him by his tribe, is a sign not only of wifely duty, but of the positive quality of their relationship. Family members do not always take seriously their relatives' religious experiences. They often demean and patronize them. But Khadija found her husband's religious instincts credible and became his first convert. In fact, his next two converts were people he knew well—a cousin, Warakh, and Zaid, a slave he had freed and adopted as a son. A few of the early converts were merchants and persons with some standing in Mecca, especially Abu Bakr of the Umayad clan, but most of his first followers were from the lower classes.

Muhammad was drawn again and again to the cave at Mt. Hira, and Gabriel kept reciting the words of Allah to him. The more Gabriel spoke, the more convinced Muhammad was that he was not mad (81:19-25). He memorized the words revealed to him and then recited them to his friends, who wrote them on any piece of scrap material they could find, be it stones, leather, leaves, or bone.

And so over a period of twenty-three years, until his death in 632, Allah, through the angel Gabriel, communicated the words of the Quran to Muhammad. For Islam this is the greatest of miracles—that an illiterate, ordinary camel-herder from Mecca could be the source of such wisdom, could remember it, and above all could recite it in such exquisite verse. It was clear to his followers that only Allah could be responsible for this.

Leader of Islam

So at age forty, Muhammad was launched on a new career. He began to teach and proclaim God's word with rhetorical eloquence notwithstanding his illiteracy. His Arab genes bestowed on him the gifts for words, poetry and story-telling.

One of the first things he did after his call was to forsake his family idols. Just as Abraham, twenty-five hundred years before, crushed his father's idols and ventured forth in the name of Allah, Muhammad renounced the numerous deities associated with his community in Mecca.

In 620 more tragedy struck the Prophet. His uncle Talib and his beloved Khadija died. The death of his wife was a particularly severe blow. They had been married for twenty-five years and in spite of the social norm of polygamy, he had been monogamous throughout their marriage. He would miss her companionship and loyalty.

Within a year or so, his family and tribe withdrew support from Muhammad and virtually disowned him. The entire Meccan community became hostile because his message threatened them in several major ways. It meant they had to forego worship of many gods; this resulted in a subsequent loss of revenue from the sale of idols representing the hundreds of deities enshrined in the Kaaba. Furthermore, his ethical demands and call for social justice challenged their self-interest. His insistence on shifting primary kinship loyalty from the tribe to the new Muslim community (umma) raised the level of ridicule to fever pitch. So in 615, to avoid being under siege, about seventy-five Muslims emigrated to Abyssinia (current Ethiopia) across the Red Sea and were protected by Negus, its pious Christian king.

Meccan citizens soon came to Negus and offered him many gifts if he would extradite the Muslims. But the apparently fair King Negus allowed a spokesman for the new religion to respond. Abu Talib made an impassioned plea, using especially Mary's Sura 19. When Negus and his advisors heard the Sura, they said: "These words must have sprung from the same fountainhead from which the words of the master Jesus Christ have sprung."[7] Rejection at the hands of Muhammad's family and friends resulted in a conspiracy to kill him. Now Muhammad was an orphan again, but this time there was a major difference. He felt Allah's support and guidance.

This threat on his life occasioned a second, more famous migration (Hegira—Hijra in Arabic) or flight to escape persecution in Mecca. On July 16, 622, Muhammad and a few hundred followers went to Yathrib, a city not quite three hundred miles north of Mecca. Actually Hegira means more than "flight." It has more to do with severing ties, leaving your tribe and making your home in another place. Now Muhammad belonged to Medina, the new name of Yathrib. It was now Madinah al-Nabi, the city of the Prophet.

This flight to Medina was so decisive a move, such a defining moment for Islam, that the Muslim calendar is dated from that activity. It was not Muhammad's birth, as in Jesus' case, which divided history, but this migration to Medina.

Why did the Hegira divide history? Why was it such a foundational event? Professor I. Abu-Rabi, Hartford Seminary's Duncan Black Macdonald teacher for the Study of Islam and Christian-Muslim Relations, suggests three reasons. In the first place, historically and politically, it meant the creation of a strong Islamic state to which Muslims could now belong. They were no longer stateless persons. They had moved from Dar al-Harb (House of War) in Mecca to Dar al-Islam (House of Peace) in Medina. Second, from a religious point of view, it meant that Muslims could freely practice their new faith and legislate for their own needs. Third, in a symbolic sense, Muslims were willing to sacrifice their former tribal and clan loyalties for their new family identity in Islam.

Relation to God had priority over past relationships. It is for these reasons that all years since the migration are "A.H." ("After Hegira").

The flight to Medina was also triggered by a civil crisis there. Muhammad had received an invitation by the city's leaders to moderate the differences among quarreling factions. Tension between local Arab families and between them and the strong Jewish community, which had been in Medina for centuries, was at a breaking point.

Muhammad was successful in drawing together the rival parties. The city became more united than it had been for years. More importantly, as we have mentioned, Islam as we know it had its formative years in Medina. The first mosque was built there; a rudimentary ritual life, which later evolved into the five pillars of faith, began there; the first call of the muezzin was heard in Medina; and the first Muslim community was formed there. In short, Islamic civilization began in Medina.

In addition to all this, under the inspiration of Muhammad, a famous covenant was made between Jews, Muslims, and other inhabitants of the city. This document, formulated by Muhammad, guaranteed religious liberty in the city and determined the rights and duties of members of all religions: Christians, Jews, Muslims, Zoroastrians, and others.

M. H. Haykal's biography of Muhammad, mentioned earlier, contains a copy of this forward-looking covenant. It is evidence of Muhammad the statesman at work. Haykal's commentary on the Charter of Medina suggests how Muhammad saw Islam transcending the human barriers of family, class, religion, and other walls of social separation.

We should briefly mention Muhammad's relationship with the Jews at the beginning of his public career. Jews in Medina eagerly anticipated his arrival in their city. They felt a natural affinity for him. Had he not included Abraham, Moses, and the Torah in his religious vision? Did he not call Jews the "People of the Book" (*Ahl al-Kitab*)? They were his brothers and sisters; to show how grateful he was for his roots in Judaism, Muslims were asked to face Jerusalem when they prayed.

This happy relationship turned sour when the Jews finally would not accept Islam and convert to the new religion as Muhammad had fully expected them to do. Jews could not acknowledge Ishmael and Jesus the way Muhammad did, and they did not find their messianic hopes fulfilled in Muhammad, this notwithstanding how much the Quran had been influenced by Hebrew scripture and tradition. They insisted that the Messiah must come from Isaac through David's line, not from the house of Ishmael. When Jews rejected his message and betrayed him in later military endeavors, Muhammad expelled them from Medina and destroyed many of them. To indicate the newly found autonomy of Islam, Muhammad further asked his followers to stop praying toward Jerusalem and turn to Mecca.

After two years of consolidating his movement and forming his Muslim community into a military and spiritual force, Muhammad felt secure enough to leave Medina and return to his hometown. On the way to Mecca he engaged in three battles which are firmly etched in the memory of Islam. The first took place in 624 at Badr, where Muhammad and his troops were attacked by the Meccans led by Abu-Jahl. The Muslims won the battle over a far superior army of the Qurasyh and believed that Allah must have intervened for them to achieve such a surprising victory. Then in 625, at the battle of Uhud, near Medina, Muhammad and the Qurasyh fought again, but this time to what at best can be called a draw. During the battle, Muhammad was physically hurt, but his pride was doubly wounded. Miraculously he made his way back to Medina. The Quran understands this setback to be a result of the soldiers' lack of faith and ad-monishes them for it (3:131). It also sets forth the notion that fighting on behalf of Allah (Jihad) assures one a place in Paradise.

Within a few years he was ready to make his return trip to Mecca. This time he was thwarted by a large Qurasyh force encamped some miles from Medina. They planned to attack the city and destroy the fledgling Muslim army. A bitter struggle was expected. However, a clever Persian, Salmon by name, advised Muhammad to dig a large ditch around Medina. The thought was that this might alleviate a major battle, a great deal of bloodshed, and a possible defeat at the hands of the Meccan tribe. When the Qurasyh leaders found the trench impassable, they eventually retreated.

As Muhammad approached Mecca in 628, he received a revelation to make a lesser pilgrimage, not a complete Hajj (48:27). But, at a nearby town of Al-Hudaybiyyah, Muhammad and about a thousand of his men were prevented from entering Mecca by the Qurasyh tribe. As a result of some negotiation, Muhammad and the Qurasyh decided to call a truce at Hudaybiyyah. This pact certainly saved many lives and displayed the peaceful intentions of Muhammad.

Under terms of the truce, Muhammad could perform his pilgrimage during the next year; there would be peace between Meccans and Muslims for ten years, and if a Qurasyh tribal member deserted to the Muslims, he would have to be returned. However, Muhammad was not granted the same privilege if a Muslim returned to join the Mecca tribe.

The Prophet did make his pilgrimage in 629. But the truce was broken by a skirmish between some Meccans and allied tribes. This became the occasion for Muhammad to move into Mecca. Finally, in 630, Muhammad and his troops were able to enter their hometown. To his surprise and great good fortune, the city which had earlier sought his death, surrendered without resistance. It was considered another of Allah's victories. Muhammad did not exploit the weakened condition of the city. He was magnanimous toward the vulnerability of his former enemies and with few exceptions, amnesty was declared for all the citizens.

The return to Mecca was Muhammad's first opportunity as a Muslim to make a pilgrimage to the Kaaba. What he did at this time became a prototype for all succeeding pilgrimages to the holy city. To the astonishment of many, he did not destroy the Kaaba. After all, it was the first house of worship built for Allah by Abraham and Ishmael, and he would give it the respect it deserved. So he rode around it seven times and acknowledged with reverence the "Black Stone" placed within its southeast corner.

But what of the 360 idols placed in the Kaaba during pre-Islamic "time of ignorance?" All of them, one by one, were withdrawn and systematically destroyed. It was the end of idolatry in Arabia. As Muhammad said, "Truth has come."

Soon after his triumph in Mecca he returned to Medina. During this visit, he developed a high fever and became deathly ill. On June 8, 632, on a reportedly scorching hot day, the Prophet died. Some say his last words, as his head lay in the lap of one of his wives, Aisha, were, "Rather God on High and Paradise."

Aisha was one of the several women Muhammad married after the death of Khadija. Many of them were marriages of mercy and out of concern for the social and economic welfare of the women. He did have one other child, a son, Ibrahim, by a Coptic woman. That son died at eleven months. Aisha, about whom we hear more than the others, was his favorite wife, after Khadija. Fatima, youngest daughter of Khadija, married Muhammad's nephew, Ali. They had two boys, Hasan and Husayn.

The Expansion of Islam

The rate of Islam's expansion after Muhammad's death has no parallel in history. Because he made his native land an Islamic country during his lifetime, the new faith burst forth from Arabia like a skyrocket. Before twenty years had elapsed, Islam spread north of Arabia to Damascus and Jerusalem, east to Persia, west to Egypt, and further on to the northern coast of Africa. This expansion included the construction of magnificent centers of Islamic culture, education, and religion in such cities as Baghdad and Cairo.

ISLAMIC CALIPHATES

Medina Caliphate	632-661
Umayyad Caliphate of Damascus	661-750
Abbasid Caliphate of Baghdad	750-1258
Umayyad Caliphate of Cordova	756-1031
Fatimid Caliphate	909-1171
Ottoman Empire of Turkey	1453-1924

By 715, a hundred years into the Islamic era, the new religion was in control of the Mediterranean Sea and the European country of Spain. If Charles Martel had not stopped the Muslim advances into southern France at Tours in 732, all of that continent might have fallen under Muslim rule. At any rate, by 800, Muslims controlled land from Switzerland to the eastern regions of India, an area larger than the Roman Empire at its zenith. In the twelfth century, this Arabian political and religious energy waned, only to return with renewed vigor in the sixteenth-century success of the Ottoman empire.

Islam tended to be viewed positively by people it conquered. This was due in some measure to the relief they felt after centuries of tyrannical rule by Byzantine emperors and Persian kings. It was also due in large measure to the sense of equality and justice found in the Quran and practiced by the Muslim rulers.

Conquered people were called Dhimmis—non-Muslims who were guaranteed tolerance by Islamic law. Jews and Christians, because of their relation to "The Book," were given special treatment. Dhimmis were permitted to retain their religious and civil rights, and for this privilege, a tax, similar to our state taxes, was levied against them.

As we know in the West, it is difficult for a colonizing power to be completely just and fair. The combination of cross and flag during 400 years of European empire building was not Christianity's finest hour. Islam, as a conquering force, did not always live up to the ideals of the Quran. But in most cases, Muslims were able to live harmoniously with their neighbors and the people they ruled.

Part Two

Essential Islam

Beliefs of Islam

The Oneness of God

La ilaha illa Allah, wa Muhammad rasul Allah
There is no god but Allah and
Muhammad is the prophet of Allah.

Say: Allah is One, the Eternal God. He begot none,
nor was he begotten. None is equal to Him. (112:1-4)

The foundation of Islam is the uncompromising unity and
oneness of God, called *Tawhid* in Arabic. Allah is beyond
distinction and division and has no equal or associate. A
poetic version of the quotation from the Quran with which
this section begins goes: "Know, child, that God is only One
and has no partner or son." (Sayyed Mohammed)

It bears repeating that for Islam Allah is not *a* god, the highest god, a supreme being or the most important god. All
these statements imply the existence of other divinities. But

the confession without which Islam cannot survive is, "There is no God but God." (2:163) This negative has the most positive effect for the Muslim's faith. In a verbal stroke, every competitor to Allah is abrogated and eliminated.

The name Allah is etymologically rooted in the oldest name for god found in ancient Babylonia; it is a root which linguistically links Judaism and Christianity to Islam. In Babylonia, the name was *il* and that later become *El* in Hebrew. That helped create Elohim, one of the Hebrew names for God. And Christians say that Jesus was Emmanu*el* which means "God with us." *El* came into Arabic with the definite article as *Il-ah* and then into English as "Allah," *the* God, literally, the one to be worshiped. So in addition to the ties which unite Judaism, Christianity, and Islam by way of a common ancestor, Abraham, we have a common bond in our names for God.

There is a sense in which the three religions are epigenetic, that is, they build on each other. Just as Christians believe that Jesus' view of God as love is a fuller understanding of God than the Jewish one of justice, so Muslims believe that the Quran's claim that God is radically One is a more complete revelation than that of Christianity. (See 2:113) There is some stereotyping in such claims by each religion. A clearer, more accurate relationship of Islam's monotheism to Judaism and Christianity is that Islam is a return to the revelation Abraham received from Allah. The Abrahamic revelation was repeated without error in the words Muhammad received from Allah: *"La ilaha illa Allah."*—"There is no God but God." This singularity, oneness, and unity of God cannot be stressed enough as we attempt to understand Islam.

Although God is One, there are many names for God. The Quran contains ninety-nine "most beautiful names of God." (7:180)

The Subha: a prayer thread consisting of thirty-three beads and a tassel. When used three times it helps the Muslim remember the ninety-nine names of God. [Photo by Mary D. Zepp.]

A short list includes the following: Creator, All-Merciful, Guardian of Faith, All-Holy, All-Wise, Just, Beautiful, Loving, Compassionate, and Glorious. For more names, see 59:22-24 and 2:255. Other names which complete the list are found in the Hadith.

Devout Muslims repeat these names as they use the *subha*, a set of prayer beads very similar to a Catholic rosary. The subha contains thirty-three beads with a tassel at the end. As the devotee runs each bead through his or her fingers, a name for God is pronounced, and by going through the chain three times, the ninety-nine names are completely remembered.

As one might suspect, the unpardonable sin in Islam is idolatry (*Shirk*). An idol is created when you call any visible thing God or when any object made with human hands is worshiped. Something less than God has replaced God. In Islamic terms, you have relativized the absolute. A creature has become the Creator.

Nothing offends Islam more than this. "Allah will not forgive idolatry. He will forgive whom He will all other sins. He that serves other gods beside Allah has strayed far from the truth." (4:48) It is precisely this tenacious monotheism which is the source of Islam's successful resistance to capitalism, communism, nationalism, and other ultimate claims. Muslims refuse to bestow adoration on anything or anyone which properly belongs to Allah. A Muslim cannot abide the thought of trivializing or devaluing God in this way.

There are several significant practical implications of Allah's Oneness.

God is never called "Father." This implies kinship ties with a wife or children; even in the general sense, human beings are not children of God. Remember there is to be no one associated with God. Further, to speak of God in human terms—such as loving Father, resting on the Sabbath, hating his enemies, having face, hands, or feet—is too anthropomorphic (God conceived in human form) and viewed with suspicion by Muslims.

It is also inappropriate to call God "father of a nation" as Jewish scriptures do. And, of course, Jesus' use of "Abba, Father" in personal prayer is incomprehensible to Muslims. "They [Christians] say: Allah has begotten a son. Allah forbid." (2:116)

Allah is the only personal name permitted for God. It has neither plural nor gender. "God" can be plural as in "gods" and feminine as in "goddess." The frequent use of the male pronoun "He" for God is a result of a longstanding tradition in monotheistic patriarchal religions. It goes without saying how difficult it is for Muslims to understand the Christian claim that Mary is the "Mother of God."

Muslims reject out of hand the Christian formula "In the name of the Father, and the Son, and the Holy Spirit," wherein God or Allah is not mentioned at all. The Muslim version would be "In the Name of God, the Most Compassionate, the Most Merciful." Allah is not the son of a father nor the father of a son. Or as the Quran says, "God is not a Third of Three." (5:76)

The Quran sees irretrievable traces of polytheism in Judaism and Christianity. Even though they purport to be monotheistic religions, Muhammad uncovers serious distortions in their good intentions.

First of all, as we mentioned earlier, one of the Hebrew words for God is *Elohim*, a plural version of *El* and literally a reference to "Gods." This is too serious a qualification of Allah's unity.

Second, it is a concern for Islam that birth into the Jewish family, rather than obedience to God, is the key to one's relationship to God. Submission to Allah's will, not biological lineage, is the predication of authentic relation to God.

In the third place, Christian prayer in the name of Jesus and belief in the Incarnation (that God became a human person in Jesus of Nazareth) compromises beyond repair the Oneness of God. You no longer have a unity of God; you have a trinity or plurality of gods. Although Jews and Christians do not see themselves as anything other than monotheists, one can see the plausibility of these arguments from an Islamic perspective.

Fourth, that Sufi Muslims, the mystical branch of Islam, can claim they reach a state of oneness with God in their ecstatic union is a scandal to orthodox believers. Some Sufis, in their unbounded enthusiasm, said they became God, that only God existed. Nothing would horrify a traditional Muslim more than to make a very close intimate relationship with God one of identity with God.

A fifth implication of God's Oneness and corresponding fear of idolatry is that no visible representation of Allah or Muhammad is allowed. Just to make sure there is no temptation to worship a human being, there are no pictures, icons, or statues in a mosque. One should never be distracted from Allah, who is at the heart of devotion. It is clear by now that no one or no thing is associated with God. God is beyond comparison.

The Unity (*Tawhid*) of Allah is reflected in the unity of Allah's creation and the order of the world. This especially means the unity of the human family. Brotherhood and sisterhood of all peoples is the logical consequence of the Unity of God; we are all related! This is the reason for the clarion call of inclusiveness in Islam and the basis of its universal appeal.

It follows that this unity of Allah helps us transcend diversity. All races, classes, ethnic groups, and nationalities are in solidarity with each other. Malcolm X discovered this with extraordinary clarity during his pilgrimage to Mecca in 1964. He perceived that the closer people of all cultures and social backgrounds got to the center, the closer they were to each other. Malcolm returned to the United States with a new vision of openness to Allah's people and an appreciation and a tolerance of difference he did not have before the trip to the sacred center. This is Islam's universalism at its best.

Furthermore, the Unity of Allah implies the unity of social, political, and religious life. The deeply held belief in one Lord and Creator means there is no dichotomy between science and religion, the sacred and the secular, church and state, or economics and religion. It is difficult for Muslims to understand how many westerners take these divisions in their national life for granted, especially those having to do with with religion and politics. To quote Jesus' words, "Render unto Caesar what is Caesar's and unto God what is God's," would not help. They see us as a secular society which has shoved God to the edge of public life or into the private spheres of our heart and soul. Neither is hardly a place for an omnipotent deity to whom we must submit and to whom we are ultimately responsible.

> God is beautiful and He loves beauty.
>
> (Muhammad)

ATTRIBUTES OF GOD

Mercy. A first-time reader of the Quran is struck by the fact that, except for one, each Sura or chapter begins with the words, "In the name of God, the Merciful, the Compassionate" or "In the name of God, most Gracious, most Merciful." This centrality of Allah's mercy serves as an antidote to the notion so prevalent in the West that Islam's God is an austere and stern judge whose awe and majesty make him unapproachable.

There are countless verses in the Quran which stress the mercy and forgiveness of Allah, "Seek forgiveness of your Lord and turn to Him in repentance. My Lord is loving and merciful." (11:90) God's mercy includes and comprehends everything, even His justice and our disobedience. Some commentators speak of the "oceanic" mercy of Allah. It is safe to say that Islam's world turns on the axis of Allah's mercy. (See 6:12, 16:5, 24:14, 33:73)

Most Christians and Jews are in agreement with this fundamental understanding of the nature of God affirmed by Islam. God is gracious, slow to anger, and eager to forgive. It is very clear in Islam, however, that God's love is not sentimental, like a river without banks. As with Christianity, God's holiness and righteousness must not be nullified with a kind of "sloppy agape."

It should be stressed that access to God's mercy is by our repentance and that alone. Allah forgives wrongdoers and will pardon any who sincerely repent and are truly sorry for violating the law of God. Although Islam is uncomfortable calling God "Father," Allah acts like a compassionate parent. A saying attributed to Muhammad states that "God is more loving and kind than a mother to her dear ones." We conclude that the primary Muslim experience of God is mercy, compassion, and forgiveness.

Justice. A secondary, but nevertheless very important, aspect of God's nature is justice. Islam believes there must be judgment for all human behavior—goodness should be rewarded and evil punished. Otherwise, the universe falls off its moral hinges. At the end of our days, there is an inevitable and fair accounting of our deeds. Without this divine reckoning, we would lack incentive to be virtuous. The righteous will be blest in a Garden of Delight, and sinners, short of repentance, can be assured of Allah's retribution. Even if He has the final say, Muslims trust Allah to be utterly fair in His execution of justice: "Allah keeps count of all things" and "He has knowledge of all things." (4:86 and 24:35) The moral ground of the universe provided by God is the basis for a just and moral Islamic social order. As God is just, we are to be just.

Creator. Allah created all that is; He contains the heavens and the earth, the east and the west. They belong to Him because He is their source. (2:115, 31:26)

The potency of Allah is evidenced by the capacity to create through speech. "To Him is due the primal origin of the heavens and the earth; when He decrees a matter, He says to it, 'Be.' And it is." (2:117) This recalls the Genesis account in which God says, "Let there be..." and whatever was to be, occurred. In the same way, Allah, by speaking, creates out of nothing.

Because God created all things, there is an order and purpose to the universe. Human beings and the natural world are not here by chance or as the Quran says, we were not "made for sport." No cosmic joke is being played on us. (44:38) We were created to live meaningfully, for example, in submission to Allah, in justice with our neighbors, and in faithful management of the earth.

Allah loves the good creation He has made. One of the most endearing of the beautiful names for Allah is "Cherisher." People and the earth are dear to Allah and He diligently nourishes and sustains them. If Allah were to cease cherishing, the cosmos would disintegrate.

Part and parcel of a belief in a transcendent Creator is that the creation is qualitatively different from the Creator. We are not extensions of Allah or of the same substance as He. We are created by Him, and by virtue of being created, we and all of the natural world are dependent, contingent, relative, and finite. This is by no means a devaluation of people and nature. As we have seen, they are good and cherished by Allah. It is to say that we cannot turn the Creator-creation structure on its head and have the creature be the Creator. This is the idolatry Islam finds taboo.

Allah the Creator is also Allah the Eternal. One of the most famous verses in the Quran is, "Allah is One, the Eternal God; He begot none nor was He begotten. None is equal to Him. He was not born nor does He give birth." (112:1-4; See also 2:255.) By virtue of being Eternal, Allah is self-starting and self-sustaining, not dependent, not subject to temporal modes of ebb and flow, waking or sleeping; He is the Everlasting One, the Beginning and the End.

But with all this emphasis on otherness, transcendence, and distance from us, Allah desires intimacy; He is closer than our bloodstream. An oft-quoted verse from the Quran (50:16) reminds us that "God is nearer than our jugular vein." It is important to remember how Islam balances the distance and nearness, the transcendence and the immanence of God.

Light. The Creator of heaven and earth is also their Light, says Sura 24:35. This statement is followed by the famous Parable of the Niche, variously called the Parable of the Lamp or the Glass. Just as a light was placed in a concave opening high on the wall of an Arabian house, just as it was surrounded by glass for protection and for passage of light to the room, God, from on high, diffuses His light through the words of the Quran and the prophets. They contain, protect, and permit the communication of God's word to people.

The prophets and the Quran are not the light, according to Yusaf Ali, but the glass through which the light shines. Hence, they do not receive praise and glory; only God, the source of Light, receives that. Our light is derived light; we let it shine so others can see the Light of the world and give the Creator credit and gratitude.

Allah, through Quranic light, guides us as we walk in darkness and confusion; it illuminates our path and enlightens our mind so we can think and speak clearly. Since the Light of God is all-pervading the Quran says that wherever you turn, you see the face of God. This "all-seeing Eye" necessarily exposes everything and documents God's knowledge of our activity. There is no hiding place down here. Allah is the unseen guest in our homes and the silent listener to our conversations. (6:3, 58:7, 3:2)

Finally, God's light will continue to shine even though we may wish to extinguish it. "Unbelievers may detest it," but they can never blow it out. (3:2, 9:32, 61:8)

Sovereignty. In one way or another, the following phrases are found in the Quran: "God guides whom He will." "Allah does what pleases Him." "Whom He permits, will be able." This is a way of saying that Allah is Lord of the world, controller of history, and determiner of our personal lives and nature's purposes. (2:255)

But this sort of language raises the age-old question which plagues monotheistic religions—the issue of predestination and free will. Strictly speaking, there is no logical path out of this dilemma. However, rather than seeing these verses as abstractions, that is, independent of human experience, Islam sees them as evidence of a rich, dynamic, and existential relationship between Allah and the believer. Allah has unlimited power, but (and the "but" is a pivotal qualifier for Islam) we are free, responsible individuals.

The focus is on our freedom, not on Allah's determinism. In the reality of our actual relation to Allah, the following paradox surfaces. On the one hand, our righteousness is our own; we have achieved it. On the other hand, we don't take credit for it; self-righteousness is condemned. It is Allah's ever available mercy which enables us to be who we are. This is the confession of a devout Muslim.

Islam has avoided the logical impasse of how an omnipotent God exists alongside our free will by declaring that Allah's power, while remaining intact, does not abrogate our freedom and moral responsibility. In fact, God wills our freedom! Nothing is more crucial in Islam.

The permissive will of Allah may allow misfortunes to come our way. These "tests" are seen as part of a bigger picture and we must trust Allah, that in His good time, here or hereafter, we will see clearly what is invisible to us now. In the meantime, we know our purpose is to be a responsible agent of God on earth.

The most helpful summary of what Muslims believe about God is found in the first Sura, called *Fatiha* or "opening." It is the central prayer of Islam and is used on all special occasions as well as during the five daily prayers. The Fatiha serves the same purpose for Muslims that the Lord's Prayer serves for Christians. Notice how it includes the main features of Muslim theology:

> In the Name of Allah the Compassionate, the Merciful. Praise be to Allah, Lord of the Creation, the Compassionate, the Merciful, King of Judgment Day! You alone we worship, and to you alone we

pray for help. Guide us in the straight path, the Path of those whom you have favored, not of those who have incurred Your wrath, nor of those who have gone astray.

Here you find gratitude and praise for the uniqueness and oneness of Allah who is our creator. Allah is a merciful God who is our Judge and alone deserves worship. The second half of the prayer asks God for illumination and guidance along the path of life, the straight path Islam has provided.

> *To thee We sent the Scripture in truth, confirming the scripture that came before it, and guarding it in safety: so judge between them by what God hath revealed and follow not their vain desires, diverging from the truth that hath come to thee.* (Sura 5:51)

Divinity of the Quran

Bismillah hir Rahman nir Rahim
In the Name of God, the Merciful, the Compassionate

No book ever commanded as wide or as deep a reverence as did the Quran; none has been copied and
recopied, passed from generation to generation,
memorized in part or in toto, recited in solemn
worship as well as in salons, marketplaces, and
schoolrooms as much as the Quran. Above all, no
book has ever been the cause of such deep religious,
intellectual, cultural, moral, social, economic, and
political change in the lives of millions, or of peoples
as ethnically diverse, as has the Quran. (Isma'il R. al-
Faruqi)

Recite! Your Lord is the Most Bountiful One, Who by
the Pen taught man what he did not know. (Sura
96:3-5)

That we are taught by "the Pen" indicates how, for Islam,
saving knowledge comes by way of a text, the Holy Quran.
Revelation from God is not through a person, but through a
written record. Islam is a Book Religion! Muslims are
sometimes called "Quranists." Therefore to be ignorant of

this book is to miss not only the message of Islam, but its heart and soul as well.

Boy reading the Quran [A Saudi Aramco Photo]

QURAN AS HOLISTIC EXPERIENCE

Muslims experience the Quran; they do not simply read it or study it, although both are stressed. The experience is a holistic one—intellectual, auditory, visual, and devotional.

Intellectually, it is read and studied by scholars, teachers, and the ordinary layperson. As an act of devotion, faithful Muslims commit it to memory. Some Muslims spend years learning how to recite the lyrical rhythms of the Quran so it can be heard. ("Al-Quran" means "the recitation" in Arabic.) These reciters enter competitions and are in demand for special Muslim celebrations, such as weddings, funerals, graduations, and circumcisions. Listening to a professional reciter is so moving that it evokes a religious and aesthetic response. Finally, the pages of many Qurans are embellished by such exquisite calligraphy that viewing them is tantamount to seeing a work of art very pleasing to the eye.

This totality of experience—eye and ear, head and heart, the cognitive and affective—only hints at the impact the Quran has on Muslims and barely scratches the depth of respect they have for their beloved book.

Why are these 114 chapters, 6,616 verses, 77,934 words, and 323,671 letters so revered? Why had 30,000 of the Prophet's companions memorized all or part of this book, about the size of the New Testament, before he died? Why have Muslims, such as Faruqi in the above quotation, exhausted their language to convey its value and meaning? Why has its text been frozen for 1400 years? Why is it memorized by each succeeding generation so that if by chance every extant copy of it were destroyed, the words would remain intact?

It is not simply because it tells us everything we need to know about God and human nature, how to treat each other, how to create a humane society, where we came from, what life's meaning is, and what our ultimate destiny will be—that is all there, to be sure. But this can be found in other sacred texts. What distinguishes the Quran is that it is the presence of God in our midst.

One way to grasp the significance of the Quran for Islam is for Christians to understand that what Jesus is for them, the Quran is for Muslims. It is the literal, infallible Word of God. "It is a transcript of Our eternal book, sublime and full of wisdom." (43:4) Most Muslims believe it to be an exact replication of the "Mother of the Book" or the "Book of Books" which forever rests by the side of Allah.

The text was sent down by God and "we [Allah] will assuredly guard it from corruption." (15:9) The second Sura begins, "There is no doubt in this Book." (2:1) It is a perfect earthly copy of original heavenly verses—the essence of God from all eternity. Its accuracy has been providentially preserved as it passed from Allah through Gabriel, through Muhammad to his scribes who wrote it on whatever was available. This is the orthodox Islamic position.

There is a minority view which states that while the Quran is the Word of God, it was a seventh-century creation for Muhammad, just as for Arian Christians, Jesus was a first-century creation and not of the essence of God from all eternity.

So we see that the Quran holds the same place in Islam that Jesus holds for Christianity. Both are considered the revelation of God on earth. When you read the Quran, it is as if God is reading to you. To insult, defame, or trivialize the Quran is to do the same to Allah. That is one profound reason why Salman Rushdie's *Satanic Verses* was so offensive to traditional Islam.

The Quran is sacred in another way. It was revealed to Muhammad in the Arabic language, which makes Arabic part of the divine revelation (*Wahy*). So fused is Allah's message with its linguistic medium, that the Quran loses its authenticity if translated into another language. To avoid even nuances of difference which might arise in translation, people must learn Arabic to receive the pure Quranic message.

Because of the organic affinity of Arabic with the divine revelation to Muhammad, Arabic has not changed since the Quranic text was completed. This makes translations fourteen centuries later much easier. It is also why Quranic Arabic remains standard Arabic, containing the norms of grammar and syntactical usage among contemporary Arabs.

So, because its content (Word of God) and the medium of revelation (Arabic language) are both considered divine, the Quran is the "standing miracle" of Islam. It follows that the text of the Quran is not subject to literary or historical criticism. The Word of God is beyond the scrutiny of human beings.

HOW DID THE QURAN COME TO BE?

Over a period of twenty-three years (610-632), from the "Night of Power" near Mecca when he first heard the word "Recite," until he died in Medina, Muhammad continued to receive words from Allah. Soon after his death, his successor, Abu Bakr collected all the revelations into one document. This one copy evolved into several "versions" as it traveled to Damascus, Basra, Kufa, and Qum. (The versions differed only in regard to conventions of recitation of a few sentences and phrases, conventions arising from differences in various Arabic dialects.) An excellent account of how the authoritative edition of the Quran came into being is recorded by Dr. Sayyid Syeed:

> The different "versions" of the Qur'an only represented dialectal variations. Caliph Uthman only retained the standard Qureshi dialect with the help of scores of huffaz (those who memorized the Quran) who were also the companions of the Prophet. The companions had memorized the revelations as they were transmitted to the Prophet. They cross-

referenced all the work from their own memory. The Quran itself was not changed; only the dialectal variations were standardized. The Quran in its present form was consolidated by the Prophet himself who put together the suras and ordered them. The record of the transmission is so complete that, if you read the Arabic text of the Quran, you would note many of the special notations like where it is suggested to bow down in humility or thankfulness, etc.[8]

So, within twenty years, under the Caliphate of Uthman, the Quran was canonized into its present form. This became the authorized version and has remained the same to this day. It was at that time, as well, that the numbering, titling, and ordering of chapters were added to the revelation.

Over the years, efforts have been made by scholars to arrange the chapters according to chronology and geography. This has not been successful. We do know that the revelations occurred in Mecca (610-622) and in Medina (622-632), but the so-called Meccan and Medina verses are found in many different Suras and in several parts of the Quran. Interpreters of the Quran have noticed that the Meccan passages tend to deal with universal ideals of justice, patience, wisdom, perseverance—all virtues of a persecuted people. They also have a good deal to do with idolatry—a persistent problem in Mecca. In short, they are prophetic in tone. The Medina verses, however, are replete with references to statecraft, politics, legislation, and the arbitration of disputes—all reflecting problems associated with the establishment of the first Islamic community.

As we have said, the Quran is divided into 114 chapters (Sura) with the longest, "The Cow," having 286 verses (Ayat) and the shortest, "Daybreak," having three verses. The word "sura" really means "step" or "gradation" by which the believer ascends closer to Allah. "Ayat" is a sign, pointing to God's revelation of wisdom and mercy.

Each sura, except Number 9, begins with the Bismillah, the core of Islamic faith: "In the Name of Allah, the Compassionate and the Merciful." A chapter title usually refers to the theme of the sura or to a word or phrase which identifies its uniqueness. Some titles are oblique. For instance, "The Cow," the second and longest sura, has only about ten verses which discuss Moses' decision to sacrifice this animal. Another sura, "Women," devotes most of its verses to subjects dealing with marriage, divorce, and the general status of women.

One important distinction should be made between the final composition of the Quran and the Bible. Whereas the Bible was written over a period of 1000 years by many different people in different places, the Quran was revealed to one person and recorded immediately by scribes over a twenty-three-year period. The Hebrew Bible was officially closed in 90 CE and the New Testament was canonized by the end of the fourth century CE, in each case several centuries after the persons and events described in their respective testaments.

During the lifetime of the Prophet, as we have noted, the Quran was officially closed and passed on verbatim to the companions of the Prophet.

Message of the Quran

FULFILLMENT OF FORMER SCRIPTURES

Several Suras state that the previous scriptures of Torah, Psalms, and the Gospel were originally authentic revelations of the Mother of the Book (43:4), and were appropriate for their historical situation. Therefore, Muslims are expected to believe in Moses, David, and Jesus, to revere all these scriptures, and to respect Jews and Christians as "People of the Book."

But according to Islam, these Scriptures fell into disuse, were misinterpreted, and were partially corrupted by translations from their original languages of Hebrew and Greek. Both Testaments are admittedly incomplete. The Quran further wonders why there is so much disagreement between Christians and Jews since their scriptures are two revelations from the same God. "The Jews say, 'The Christians have nought to stand upon,' and the Christians say 'The Jews have nought to stand upon.' Yet they profess to study the same Book." (2:113)

The Quran sees itself as confirming the intentions of all these scriptures. It wants to return to the purity of pre-Torah religion, that is, Abrahamic Islam. It desires, once and for all, to clarify, complete, and universalize his vision and to insist that the Quran is responsible for the safekeeping of God's Word.

SUMMARY OF QURANIC BELIEFS

The message of the Quran can be summarized as follows:

1. The Oneness and Unity of God
2. The Mercy and Compassion of God
3. The Authenticity of Muhammad as a Messenger of God
4. The Unity of the Message delivered by earlier prophets like Adam, Noah, Abraham, Moses and Jesus
5. The Final Accountability of our Deeds
6. The Ethical Guidance for Personal Morality and Social Justice
7. The Resurrection, Last Judgment, and After-Life

(You will note that Part Two expands on each of these beliefs at some length.)

It is widely accepted by Muslims that Sura 2 is the Quran in miniature. Since every theme mentioned above is found in this chapter, the Quran is seen as a commentary on this, the longest of the Suras. In turn, the Fatiha or Sura 1, is a distillation of Sura 2. Appropriately, Fatiha literally means "key"; it opens the door to the Quran, leading us to all its basic beliefs. It serves also as the Muslim's perfect prayer; it is said several times during daily prayers and at various ritual events. In terms of popularity and frequency of usage, it is often compared to the Christian's Lord's Prayer.

Likewise, the essence of the Fatiha is found in the Shahadah, the central Muslim confession: "There is no God, but God; and Muhammad is the Prophet of God." This is the Apostles' Creed of Islam.

The pervasiveness and influence of the Quran is unavoidable in the daily life of the Muslim. It is used in daily prayers, and the Friday noon-day liturgy; it is memorized and recited for devotional purposes and always heard at rites of passage and other celebrative occasions.

Prophethood of Muhammad

From the point of view of comparative studies and the history of religion, we consider Muhammad the founder of Islam. But as we have seen, Muslims believe Allah founded Islam with Muhammad as the human instrument to proclaim its message and to implement its success.

In an earlier chapter, we presented the historical life of Muhammad. Here we want to examine the religious and theological significance of Muhammad for the faith of the average Muslim.

THE MORE THAN HUMAN
AND LESS THAN DIVINE PROPHET

M. H. Haykal summarizes well the feeling Muslims have for the Prophet:

> He became a messenger of his Lord, calling men unto Him, protecting the new faith and guaranteeing the freedom and security of its preachers. He became the ruler of the Ummah of Islam, its commander in war and teacher, judge, and organizer of all the internal and foreign affairs. Throughout his career he established justice and reconciled hopelessly desperate and hostile nations and groups. His wisdom, farsightedness, perspicacity, presence of mind, and resoluteness are evident in all that he said or did. From him streams of knowledge have sprung and heights of eloquence have arisen to which the great bend their heads in awe and wonder. He departed from this world satisfied with his work, assured of God's pleasure and crowned with the gratitude of men.[9]

The humanity of Muhammad is central to Islam. He is not divine or even the shadow of God on earth. The Prophet himself goes to great lengths to persuade us of his humanity. The Quran records that he asked forgiveness of sins. Once, Allah rebuked him for being more interested in explaining the Quran to people than helping a poor blind man. (80:1-15)

People often asked Aisha how the Prophet lived at home. "Like an ordinary man," she answered. "He would sweep the house, stitch his own clothes, mend his own sandals, water his camels, milk the goats, help the servants at their work, and eat his meals with them, and he would go to fetch a thing we needed from the market."[10] No doubt he was good at bargaining with the bazaar merchants. A typical verse in the Quran reinforces Muhammad's insistence on his humanity: "Muhammad is no more than an Apostle." (3:144) The implication is very clear: Human beings, even Apostles of God, come and go, but Allah remains forever. Don't focus on an Apostle, whether he be Moses, Jesus, or Muhammad.

These disclaimers notwithstanding, Muhammad was much more than an ordinary man, perhaps more than an Apostle. In the eyes of pious Muslims he often crossed the line from being a vehicle of God to being a perfect man.

Miracles were attributed to him just as they were to Moses and Jesus because for Islam, a true prophet is granted divine dispensation to perform signs and wonders. At one level, popular piety has pebbles talking in his hands, trees bowing as he walks by, and his body not casting a shadow. But more importantly, within mainstream Islam, there are several ways Muhammad is portrayed as a unique and extraordinary human being.

1. He was chosen to receive Allah's final revelation of scripture. Moses was given the Torah; David, the Psalms;

Jesus, the Gospel; and of course, Muhammad was given the Quran. The latter is the "Standing Miracle" of Islam and remains a living testimony to the religious genius of Muhammad and his sheer trust in God.

2. In his famous "Night Journey to Heaven" Muhammad was taken from Mecca to Jerusalem and from a rock on Mt. Zion ascended to the seventh heaven. On that flight he talked with Biblical prophets such as Moses and Abraham. While there he had a glorious vision of Allah. The Dome of the Rock in Jerusalem enshrines the place from which Muhammad, by wings of the spirit, made his divine visitation. One practical result of this spiritual trip was Muhammad's instruction to pray five times a day—a subsequent pillar of Islam.

3. According to Islamic tradition, Muhammad was foretold in Hebrew scriptures. For many Muslim scholars, Isaiah 42 predicts the coming of a servant who is associated with Kedar (Qaydar), one of Ishmael's sons whose tribe survived in Arabia (Isaiah 42, 21:13-17). That servant who is to appear in Arabia is believed to be Muhammad.

Some Muslim interpreters see Haggai 2:7 "And the treasure [desire] of all nations will come" as a promise of the advent of Muhammad. The treasure (*Himada* in Hebrew) is closely rooted to the Arabic *hemed*. This is personalized in the Arabic proper name Ahmed, an abbreviation of Muhammad, and strongly suggests a continuity with this Old Testament reference. Haggai said that the Himada would bring Shalom, and Muhammad did precisely that with his message of Islam.

Professor Abdul-Ahad Dawud further intimates that the Spirit (Paraclete) whom Jesus promised as our Advocate and who would lead us to truth is none other than Muhammad. Muslim scholars argue that the words *paraklytos,* the Comforter, and *periklutos,* one who is famous or illustrious, like Muhammad, have been used interchangeably in manuscripts as late as the fourth century.[11] From this point of view, Jesus foretold the coming of Muhammad. Another Quranic verse (61:6) ascribed to Jesus validates Muhammad's special character: "I am sent forth to you by Allah to confirm the Torah already revealed and to give news of an apostle that will come after me whose name is Ahmed."

Furthermore, Muslims believe that the Quran contains Abraham's prediction that Arabia would be the place of Muhammad's appearance. "Lord, send forth to them an apostle of their own who shall declare to them your revelation and instruct them in the Scriptures and in wisdom and purify them of sin." (2:129) It is obvious that Islam sees Muhammad in the long history of salvation outlined in Hebrew and Christian scriptures.

4. No picture of Muhammad is allowed. There is enough "sanctity" in the extraordinariness of his humanity that he could have become an object of worship, so no representation of his image is permitted. It would be a graven image

which might distract the viewer from the ultimate holiness of Allah.

5. The name of Muhammad is always followed by a benediction (word of blessing) when spoken or written by a devout Muslim. That benediction is "Peace Be Unto Him" (P.B.U.H.). To add to his significance, such phrases as "Glory of the Ages," "Peace of the World," and "Prophet of the Great Completion" are just three of the more than two hundred titles and names by which Muhammad is known. In fairness, "Peace Be Unto Him" is used after the mention of any prophet, including Jesus.

6. Some followers were shocked into disbelief when Muhammad's death was announced. Omar, a loyal companion, would not accept the fact of his mortality. He thought God took Muhammad into heaven much in the same manner as Jesus and Enoch were taken there. It was another faithful disciple, Abu Bakr, who finally persuaded Omar and others that the Prophet was, indeed, dead. He quoted the Quran: "Muhammad has died, but Allah lives."

All the above indicates that Muhammad, while not being divine or actually worshiped, is held in high esteem and venerated as the model of what every Muslim hopes to be. Perhaps this is why "Muhammad" is the most popular name for Muslim boys.

THE NATURE OF PROPHETHOOD

Islam is the quintessential prophetic religion. It believes Allah has provided every nation with prophets to bring His message for it would be unjust for Allah to require accountability of all people if they did not know what Allah expected of them. This knowledge is the heart and soul of the prophetic message.

Prophets are moral and intellectual leaders and the personification of righteousness. That is why Muslims reject such Biblical stories as drunken Lot's having sex with his daughters and David's affair with Bathsheba and the subsequent cover-up by sending her husband, Uriah, to the front lines in battle.

Prophethood is such an indispensable aspect of Islam that it is the only western religion to affirm the message of all God's prophets. The Quran is quite clear about this:

> We believe in Allah and that which is revealed to us; we believe in what was revealed to Abraham, Ishmael, Jacob, and the tribes; to Moses and Jesus and the other prophets. We make no distinction between any of them, and to Allah we have surrendered ourselves. (2:136)

This simply means you cannot be Muslim without believing in Moses and Jesus!

Islam fully understands the meaning of prophethood conveyed by the Hebrew *nabi*, the Greek *prophetes,* and the Arabic *rasul*. Neither of them has to do, primarily, with fortune telling, crystal balls, or prophesying the future. Each means telling forth, speaking on behalf of God, and interpreting the meaning of the present in the light of God's will. The prophet brings the Word of God; he is not the Word. So prophets are human beings with a divine message. This is why, for Islam, prophet is the noblest title a person can achieve.

Actually, the Quran's list of prophets is much longer than the Christian's. It mentions over twenty-five prophets; four are Arabs, three are from the New Testament—Zechariah, John the Baptist, and Jesus—and the rest are from the Old Testament. As the Quran suggests in 40:78: "We sent messengers before you: of them are those We have mentioned to you and of them are those We have not mentioned to you...." Also verse 35:24: "And to every nation we have sent a warner (a prophet)." From this long list, Islam has chosen six main Biblical prophets and given them honorary names. Six of them that are most generally agreed on by Muslim scholars are shown in the table that follows.

Biblical Prophet	Honorary Name
1. Adam	the Chosen of Allah
2. Noah	the Preacher of Allah
3. Abraham	the Friend of Allah
4. Moses	the Speaker of Allah
5. Jesus	the Word of Allah
6. Muhammad	the Apostle of Allah

Muhammad is not a savior, redeemer, mediator, messiah, or Son of God. He is the Prophet, Apostle, Messenger, Emissary, and Spokesman of God. He is the Rasul, someone not only who speaks on behalf of God, but one who is called and sent by God to bring a special revelation.

If we examine the classic understanding of a prophet, we can see that Muhammad fits every description.

1. God's word comes to the prophets in visions and moments of highest and most sublime spirituality.

2. They have a mandate from God to speak; they are constrained and impelled against their better judgment to be prophetic. In fact, they wonder why, of all people, they have been called. This reluctance and accompanying sense of personal inadequacy are often tests of a true prophet. As a result of this divine vocation, those called become transformed individuals who are confident and passionate spokesmen for God.

3. The prophet is concerned about the distance between what ought to be and what is. Consequently, the issue of ethics and social justice is addressed. This becomes a central plank in the platform of the prophet's written and spoken word.

4. Most prophets speak of impending doom. We are warned of the ultimate either-or which awaits us at the end of our life—Heaven or Hell, the Garden or the Fire. Allah has

prepared a Day of Reckoning for us all, a time of strict accountability.

5. God alone is the object of our loyalty and trust. This theme reverberates throughout the entire Bible. Israel's Shema: "Hear, O Israel, the Lord our God, the Lord is One." Elijah's retort to Ahab: "If the Lord be God, serve Him, If He be Baal, serve Him." Jesus' reply to Satan: "You shall worship the Lord your God and Him only shall you serve." Islam's Shahadah repeats the theme with unmistakeable force: "There is no God but God, and Muhammad is the Prophet of God." Prophets remind us of our first covenant with God and our tendency to forget Him. (See 7:172 and 89:15-34.) Prophethood and radical monotheism are inseparable.

Muhammad embodied all these aspects of what a prophet does and says. He experienced immediate access to God and heard God's voice clearly call him to mission. His message combined the oneness of God, an ethical imperative, and the coming divine judgment.

MUHAMMAD: THE SEAL OF THE PROPHETS

Islam believes that prophets are sent only when there is a need for them. They are especially needed when Tawhid, God's Oneness and Unity, are challenged and when previous revelations have been corrupted. From the point of view of the Quran, the time was ripe for another and final prophet. Muhammad came with the same authority as Moses and the

Torah, and as Jesus and the Gospel. Thus, he did not see himself as bringing anything new; his vocation from Allah was to confirm all previous revelations, to correct the abuses into which the religion of Moses and Jesus had fallen, and to restore the original message revealed to Abraham, the religion of Islam.

The Quran sees the Jews reducing the universal monotheism of Abraham to the "God of our Fathers" and to the "chosenness" of their people. We have already seen how the Quran views Christian Trinitarianism as an expression of polytheism. The ethnocentric monotheism of Judaism and the worship of Jesus, and to a lesser degree, the Holy Spirit, called for prophetic critique and correction.

Which is to say, Muhammad is the Seal of the Prophets—the last, the final messenger from Allah (33:40). Muhammad supersedes all previous revelations and prior prophets. Jesus is considered the most significant Prophet in the Quran next to Muhammad, but Jesus is only one in a succession of Prophets, of which Muhammad is the culmination. Just as Christians seal the canon of Scripture, that is, no more books will be added to the Bible, Islam seals forever the canon of prophethood with Muhammad.

The Quran summarizes Muhammad's prophethood in this way: "Prophet, we have sent you forth as a witness, a bearer of good news, and a warner, one who shall call men to Allah by His leave and guide them like a shining light." (33:45)

The Prophet's Mosque in Medina. It is the site of
Muhammad's tomb and the second holiest shrine in Islam.
[Photo courtesy of Aramco World]

The Wisdom of the Law

It is universally recognized that helping the weak, the underprivileged, and the deprived and seeking voluntarily to improve the quality of life for all is an objective of human morality. Few cultures, however, have sought to institutionalize it and none to legislate it.
(I. R. al-Faruqi)

The Islamic state fulfills this mandate by implementing its three-fold purpose for existence:

1. to secure the welfare of the Muslim community;

2. to call all people to submit to Allah's will;

3. to see that all human and natural life reflects Allah's intention for a world of peace and justice.

All of this is accomplished by the Shariah, or Islamic law.* It comprises the whole corpus of Islamic jurisprudence which is the authoritative guide for the Muslim's behavior. The Shariah is comprehensive and all-embracing, covering every aspect of life, such as moral obligation, legal (including civil, criminal, and ecclesiastical) guidance, ritual life, social

---

*I am indebted to Ismail R. al-Faruqi's excellent chapters on Sunna, Hadith, and Law in *The Cultural Atlas of Islam*, MacMillan Publishing, New York, 1986.

responsibility, international politics, and personal relationships.

It is important to note that Islam legislates for the personal and social dimensions of life, something many religions fail to do or are unable to do.

Equity in the courts, the rights of minorities, legal autonomy for non-Muslim groups, and being innocent until proven guilty are essential ingredients in the Shariah. This legal system outlines five categories of behavior: 1) obligatory, 2) recommended, 3) prohibited, 4) disapproved, and 5) indifferent. What appears to be a legalistic code is in fact highly flexible and always applied with mercy. With this multi-faceted approach, the Shariah attempts to provide the Islamic community with prescriptive and normative guidance for a just society. A Muslim once said that Jesus told us to love and be just; the Shariah tells us how.

What constitutes the Shariah? There are four sources which make up the Shariah and which give Islamic legal process validity: The Quran (Scripture), Hadith (Tradition), Ijma (Consensus), and Qiyas (Reason). The first two are the most important and the most utilized.

QURAN—SCRIPTURE

In an earlier section, we stressed the indispensability of the Quran for Islam and its infallibility as a guide for Muslims. It is the primary source of law and while Muhammad was alive he was its only trustworthy interpreter. He had heard the words firsthand, knew their meaning, and his continued inspiration allowed him to state reliably how the Quran should be applied to everyday situations.

But when he died, a crisis arose. Now that the Prophet had gone and revelations had ceased, who had the answers? What if the Quran does not address a problem we now face? What will be our source of guidance? To whom or what shall we turn when we are in doubt about issues? What about particular cases for which there are no known precedents? How can we apply the sometimes abstract and general instruction of the Quran to a concrete situation? How are we to act in this trading deal, or write this contract, or judge this crime? These were real questions for Muhammad's followers; they wanted desperately to embody the standards of the Quran and to approximate the ideals of the Prophet's life. This gave rise to the Hadith.

HADITH—TRADITION

For twenty-three years, between the revelations he periodically received, the Prophet said or did many things his companions and disciples wanted to remember and to emulate. These words, teachings, and deeds of the Prophet are found in the Hadith, a word which literally means "speech," or "report."

The extra-Quranic activity and sayings of Muhammad were collected into a body of tradition called Sunna, which means "example" or "path" or "custom." Often Sunna and Hadith are used interchangeably when they refer to an act or word of Muhammad. We will use the word Hadith because of the widespread employment of that word in Muslim discussion of the Law.

The Hadith is second only to the Quran in the Islamic hierarchy of authority. Since the Hadith contains the words and deeds of Muhammad and since the Quran requires all Muslims to follow his example, the Hadith was invested with a semi-sacred aura. No piece of Islamic literature has been so thoroughly examined to prove its reliability.

The content of the Hadith can be summarized under four categories.

1. Liturgical and ritual. It is a source for the worshiping life of the Muslim, with special attention to prayer, the essential aspect in worship (Salat).

2. Muhammad's role as Warner. The Prophet was called to warn people of God's eventual judgment of their lives. Many sayings in this vein are found in the Hadith. In addition, you find here how Muhammad relates his missionary work to the non-Islamic world.

3. Material about Muhammad's life as husband, father, and other personal relationships to friend and neighbor. We note in these relationships a consistent integrity, honesty, and fairness.

4. Muhammad as businessman, statesman, warrior, and leader of the community. The Hadith contains several stories about the humanity and wisdom of his leadership.

Here are examples of the Prophet's sayings and deeds found in the Hadith. Before quoting them, the speaker often says "As the Prophet said," or "As the Messenger of God said":

a. "Whoever relieves a human being from grief in this world, God will relieve him from a grief on the Day of Judgment."

b. "None of you is a true believer in Islam until and unless he loves for his fellowman what he loves for his own self."

c. "The ink of the scholar is holier than the blood of the martyrs."

d. "God said, 'Heaven and earth cannot contain me, but the heart of my devotee ever contains me.' "

e. Here is an anecdote from the Muhammad's youth which illustrates not only his wisdom, but the esteem in which he was held by his people even before his mission. On one occasion, the Kaaba had been destroyed by a severe desert storm and the issue centered around which tribe would replace the precious Black Stone in the Kaaba wall after its reconstruction. Muhammad's suggestion, which seemed to carry the day, was to place the Stone in a piece of cloth and have all four tribes carry it to its place in the wall.

But what about accuracy of this oral tradition? Every care was taken to verify the authenticity of a saying or a deed of Muhammad. Scholars, especially trained for such careful examination, would trace back a statement through a chain of reporters and until they ended with the Prophet himself, they were not satisfied. The chain of reporting would be something like this: "My father was told by his father who was told by his uncle who heard it first from the Prophet." The reporter's character was then scrutinized for moral lapses, level of maturity, and criminal behavior. Examiners would often travel thousands of miles to confirm a link in the chain.

Once the Hadith's transmission was authenticated, its content was tested. It could not contradict the content, letter, and spirit of the Quran. Furthermore, the Hadith under question must reflect the Prophethood of Muhammad, his Rasul, not his humanity.

The point here is that the Quran judges the trustworthiness of the Hadith. For example, there was a Hadith which criticized the use of silver and gold and suggested asceticism as the norm for a Muslim's life. But, seen in the light of Quranic affirmation of this world's goods and yet under appropriate stewardship of our possessions, wealth has a proper place in our lives; thus this Hadith was excluded from the collection of authentic sayings.

Within two centuries of the Prophet's death, thousands of Hadith were in general circulation. They all had to be appraised, classified, edited and grouped in the following way to determine their validity for Muslim use:

1. authoritative—bears full weight of examination

2. good—likely to be authoritative

(Legal briefs and moral guidance based on the two above-listed criteria are binding.)

3. weak—not likely to be authentic and not binding; but could be recommended

4. forged and therefore dismissed as Hadith

As a result of this meticulous research and ruthless investigation, two of the most famous Muslim scholars, Al Bukhari and Muslim (his name) included about 6,000 Hadith in their collections of authoritative Hadith. They rank very near the Quran in terms of infallible guidance for Muslim life. The authentic Hadith number in the tens of thousands, though often the numbers quoted are in the hundreds of thousands for the reason that many Hadith were transmitted by different narrators, and thus counted as separate Hadith even though the actual content, or saying of the Prophet, was the same.

In summary, we can say: The Quran tells us we should pray. The Hadith shows us how. The Quran tells us to fast. The Hadith gives us the details of Ramadan. The Quran is the

Truth and Word of God; the Hadith is the wisdom and example of the Prophet Muhammad. The Hadith helps us implement the ideals proclaimed by the Quran and flushes out what is implied or neglected by that original Revelation.

In case the Quran and Hadith prove unresourceful for satisfactory legal and moral decision-making, two other avenues are open to the Muslim jurist.

QIYAS—REASON*

Qiyas is the use of human reason in religious matters. This personal reasoning can take the form of calculation, logic, or analogy. All of this may help a Muslim face a brand new situation or determine which is the lesser of two evils in a particular case not covered in the Quran or Hadith. Since Islam respects the rational capacity of human beings, this creative intellectual effort is expected.

If, generation after generation, there were consistencies by scholars in the employment of their reason in certain legal areas, that decision would constitute a precedent. This is very close to the fourth ingredient in Shariah.

---

*Ijtihad is the whole process of legal interpretation of Quranic texts or the exercises of reason through analogy. Qiyas and Ijma are expressions of Ijtihad.

IJMA—CONSENSUS

Ijma, as a norm of legal guidance, means consensus or general agreement over a point or disputation by aging scholars, called the Ulema. Dissenting views are possible, but majority opinions carry the day. This agreement could, over a period of time, become a matter of law. Confidence in achieving unanimity is based on a Hadith in which the Prophet said, "My community will never agree on an error."

As you can see, Muslims have developed a science of how to arrive at legal and moral decisions. This passion for moral guidelines underscores Islam's stress on deeds and just how practical Islam tends to be.

For centuries, most Middle Eastern countries employed some form of European jurisprudence—either English Natural Law or the Napoleonic Code. Shariah Law is only practiced in Saudi Arabia, Sudan and some Gulf States today. With the influence of western values, it is next to impossible to universally practice Shariah Law.

The Inevitability of the Last Judgment
"The Final Weighing of Deeds"

Except for the theme of monotheism, the Quran speaks more of the coming Day of Judgment than any other topic. Confessing the Shahadah, "There is no God but God and Muhammad is the Prophet of God," and believing in the accountability of all humans before God are the cement which holds Islam together.

Among other things, Muhammad came to warn us of a time when Truth would be known, when the thoughts and intentions of the heart would be revealed. He earnestly proclaimed as inevitable a Day when accounts would be settled and when scales would be balanced.

> O God, if I worship Thee in fear of Hell,
> Burn me in Hell.
> If I worship Thee in hope of Paradise,
> Exclude me from Paradise.
> But if I worship Thee for Thine Own Sake,
> Withhold not from me Thine eternal beauty.
>
> (Attributed to an eighth-century Muslim woman named Rabia)

Fazlur Rahman, in an oblique paraphrase of Sura 50:22, said that Judgment Day is the "Hour when every human will be shaken into a unique and unprecedented self-awareness of his deeds; he will squarely and starkly face his own doings, not-doings, and mis-doings and accept the judgment upon them...."[12]

Something like a Final Judgment or Day of Reckoning is a natural corollary of monotheism. If there is One God who knows all and sets standards of behavior for the world, there must be a time of judgment or the edifice crumbles of its own weight.

Our purpose in this world is to serve God and to create a more just society. To the extent that purpose is thwarted, denied, or fulfilled by us is the extent of the severity of the judgment we will receive. So for Islam, how we respond to Allah's will is a matter of life or death.

The Quran refers to this time in various ways: Day of Retribution, Day of Wrath, Day of Decision, Day of Truth, and Day of Muster. The last predicts a time when all nations will assemble before the Judge's Throne for the "weighing of deeds."

The image of scales appears to be a direct reference to pagan Meccan commercial life in which scales were not always balanced. They often were tilted in favor of the merchant. Muhammad and the Quran call for a time when "weighing and measuring" will be done with ultimate fairness and objectivity.

A discussion of the Last Judgment provides an opportunity to see what Islam believes about Eschatology, that is, Last Things, such as Resurrection and Judgment Day, and Heaven and Hell.

RESURRECTION AND JUDGMENT DAY

For Islam, Resurrection and Judgment Day are practically the same idea and refer to the same event. We are raised from the dead to be present at Judgment Day. This day is preceded by a time of turbulence and terror. Suras 82 and 84 describe in great detail these scenes of apocalyptic doom. They are ominously entitled "Cleaving Asunder" and "The Cataclysm," respectively.

There will be natural disasters affecting the stars, sky, and oceans; graves will be opened; chaos will abound. (84:1-2) But this is only the prelude to the final terror of the Day itself. In that awe-full moment we stand alone before God, knowing what deeds we have sent forward and which ones we have kept back (82:5). We will see our slightest (an "atom's weight") good and our slightest evil in bold relief. (99:6-7) Unresolved disputes will be decided on that day by the Final Arbiter who knows everything. All issues of truth and justice will be clarified. Even what religion is the true one will be determined on that Day by Allah who "is the witness of all things." (22:17)

We should not be alarmed at how God weighs and measures our deeds. Everything we have done or said, large and small, is recorded. Our whole life will be reviewed. There are no death-bed conversions in Islam; Allah will not indulge in cheap grace or permit exploitation of His propensity to pardon. (4:18, 10:90-91)

The fate of each man is bound about his neck. "On the Day of Resurrection We shall confront Him with a book spread wide open, saying, Here is your book; read it. Enough for you this day that your own soul should call you to account." (17:13-14)

The questions are: Do our good deeds outweigh our evil ones? Were we believers or infidels? Did our actions match our confession? Were we mindful of the overlooked and disadvantaged people around us? Was our goodness for ourselves or for our neighbor?

Since Islam believes our earthly life is a loan from Allah, our actions have to prove us worthy of this divine loan; you could say that our "Islam," our submission to Allah's will, redeems that loan.

Then the Judge will see how the scales are tipped. If, "on balance," our righteousness surfaces, we will dwell in the Garden; if not, we spend the after-life in the Fire.

HEAVEN AND HELL

The primary metaphor for the place of reward is "Garden" and the prevailing image for the place of punishment is "Fire." Only Dante, who, incidentally, borrowed heavily from Islamic poets, describes the horrors of hell in more vivid detail than the Quran. However Islam's portrait of heaven is far more interesting and seductive than the Paradise of Dante.

According to the Quran, when the righteous arrive at the Garden of Bliss, they will have continuously flowing streams, perpetually clean water, a permanent oasis, rivers of milk that never sour, fountains of honey, luscious fruit of all kinds, and for men, beautiful virgins (houris). (See Suras 3:14-15, 47:15, and especially Section 3 of Sura 55.)

The unrepentant, unbelievers, and idolaters find themselves in hell where there are "chains, yokes, and a blazing fire." Here they will wear garments of liquid pitch and their faces will be covered with fire. (See Suras 14:50 and 76:4.) As they were chained to self-interest, yoked with pride, and bound with indifference to the needy in this life, they will be fitted with the same instruments of torture in the next. A story from the Hadith indicates that it is not so much that Allah sends us to hell; we make the path there ourselves: "When asked why they were sent to Hell, the sorrowful souls would say, 'It is because we were not of those who prayed, fed the poor, and accepted the Day of Reckoning.' "

Obviously for many Muslims, these images of the after-life are symbolic. They attempt to picture the other-world, a world beyond sense perception, in terms of this world, a world we see and feel. For other Muslims, the descriptions of the Garden and the Fire are taken literally. Still other Muslim scholars, F. Rahman among them, warn us that even if the punishment of hell and the joys of heaven are understood as "spiritual" states, we should not conclude that the physical is completely negated. There is no purely spiritual nor purely physical pain. Muslims do not divide the person into body and soul. We are spiritual-corporeal units, when one part of us hurts, we all hurt. In each case, metaphorically or literally, these images evoke sympathy and intend to modify our behavior accordingly.

We should hasten to say that not all Muslims see the pleasures of heaven and the pain of hell as a carrot and stick for ethical behavior. This is spiritual immaturity. We should be good for the sake of goodness and follow Allah for the intrinsic worth of doing His will. Sura 76:9 says: "We feed you [the indigent, orphan, captives] for the sake of God alone. No reward do we desire from you, nor Thanks." In fact, good works are like the Pillars of Islam; they are performed as acts of worship, as offerings to Allah.

The picturesque language which portrays the Garden and the Fire are ways Islam stresses the importance of submission to the will of God. Striving to be morally responsible and socially just in this life helps us prepare for the next. Heaven and hell are pre-existent in how these ultimate values are played out in our lives and relationships. Our future is being determined by our actions now.

The Protection of the Angels

The significant role played by the angel Gabriel in communicating the Quran to Muhammad is a sign of how important angels are for the religion of Islam. Gabriel, whom Muslims believe appeared to Moses and to the Virgin Mary, is considered the supreme angel and his activity is the model of angelic ministry. He acted as an agent of Allah to perform a specific duty.

These invisible beings are assigned particular tasks by God and are endowed with the necessary spiritual power to fulfill those assignments. This means they are not free as human beings are; they are bound to do the will of God. In the Quranic version of the Creation story, angels are asked to bow before Adam and Eve because they had the courage to accept the burden of free will. And because of this moral capacity, humans have a higher status than angels.

Nevertheless, angels have several important missions.

1. God has appointed angels to protect us in much the same way as the West understands the work of guardian angels. "We are your protectors in this life and in the hereafter." (41:31) (See also 82:10-12) However, with their free will, human beings can reject or accept the blessing and warning the angels bring.

2. It is Islamic tradition that each of us at birth is assigned two angels—one to record our good deeds and one to record our bad ones. Sura 82 goes on to say that these kind and honorable spirits know and understand all that we do. They accompany us through our life's journey and finally go with us to the Throne of Judgment for the final accountability of our lives. Of course, Allah knows our deeds; the angels' recording is for our benefit and to assure us that justice is being done by Allah.

3. Angels are bearers of courage. When we are in distress and weakness, "angels descend [and say] fear not, nor

grieve. But receive the good tidings." (41:30) Muhammad felt that angels encouraged him and his soldiers in the early battle with the Meccans. Countless Muslims since have testified how angelic visitors brought them comfort and strength.

Monotheistic deities tend to surround themselves with helpers and assistants who are delegated work to do on God's behalf.

The Positive Nature of Human Beings

SIN = FORGETFULNESS
SALVATION = REMEMBRANCE

Islam has a realistic view of human nature, that is, it is at the same time pessimistic and optimistic about our ability to be merciful and righteous. This realism is based on the Creation story in the Quran. The classic verses are in Sura 15: "We created man from sounding clay, from mud molded into shape." (26) And almost immediately Allah continues, "[I] breathed into him My Spirit." (29) (See also 6:2 and 7:12.)

The "breath of God" establishes our distinctiveness among created things. We have been given rational faculties and a longing for God which animals and the rest of nature do not possess.

Here is our misery ("mud") and our grandeur ("Allah's Spirit"), our bondage to this world and our capacity to soar to heights of excellence. The emphasis in Islam, however, falls on the positive, on our ability to perform God's will. The Quran is aware of our lapses and weakness, but it is more conscious of our dignity, value, and worth.

This realistic combination of egoism and altruism means that we are not naturally inclined to good or evil, but to both. In Islam we are not original sinners or original saints. As a result of our actions we become either. Sin is not who we are, but what we do. It is an act of disobeying God's law, a transgressing of the bounds set by God, or more importantly, sin is an act of forgetting God.

One Muslim scholar clearly states Islam's denial of original sin: "To say that a man is sinful even before he has committed a sin and that every child is born with a depraved nature, inherently and utterly incapable of avoiding sin would be an aspersion upon the Creator." (See U. A. Samad's *A Comparative Study of Christianity and Islam,* pp. 95-96.)

There is no "fall" from grace in Islam, but there is what might be called "a descent" from one realm to another. This happens as a result of Satan (Iblis), who wants us to have amnesia about Allah. The Devil tempted Adam and Eve to eat of the "Tree of Eternity" and in that act of disobedience, our first parents forgot the Oneness of God and made themselves their sole authority. In Islam "forgetfulness" of God always precedes disobedience.

After yielding to the Devil's bidding, Adam and Eve are cast "down" to earth, for the Garden of Eden is not on earth as in the Hebrew story, but in a higher realm, transcending this world. When they realize the consequences of their actions, they throw themselves on the mercy of God, asking forgiveness. God immediately grants them merciful pardon. It is important to note here that for Islam the major responsibility for Adam's sin does not lie with Adam or Eve, but with the Devil who tempted them.

That Adam and Eve were forgiven means sin does not forever condemn us, nor force us constantly to return to ground zero. Progress in the moral and religious life is expected.

Another profound result of the Islamic view of human nature is the elimination of the need for a Savior or Redeemer. A doctrine of Atonement is unnecessary. No one can save us from our sin; only we can do that by sincere repentance and an improved life.

The word "salvation" is not found in the Quran and is a word seldom used by Muslims. They rather talk of "success" or "achievement," that is, success in achieving Paradise. This is not a haughty or self-righteous claim; it is only to say that Muslims struggle (Jihad) to measure up to the example of Muhammad and to follow the path outlined in the Quran. The models of the prophet and the scripture are not beyond our reach. Allah would not expect of us what we are not capable of achieving.

The burden of sin or "forgetfulness" is ours and in our struggle to "remember" we find the supporting mercy of Allah. So we are "saved" or achieve Paradise by faithfully "remembering" Allah and His commands. Muslims remind us that in the Gospels, Jesus said Eternal Life comes from "keeping the commandments." (Matthew 19:17) In the same way belief and good works unite to guarantee "success" for a Muslim: "Yet to those of them who embrace the Faith and do good deeds He has promised forgiveness and a rich reward." (Quran 48:29; see also 2:112, 3:130-136.)

In summary, Islam believes human beings are relatively good, radically free, and capable of change. Allah is bound to respect these marks of our humanity. These traits—goodness, freedom, and capacity—have as their goal what we would call an integrated person, someone in whom there is the least amount of distance between what is said and what is done, whose profession becomes practice. This is the example Muhammad set for Muslims.

HUMAN BEINGS AS DEPUTIES OF GOD

Allah respected men and women so much that He made them His "vicegerents" (2:30), which means we have the awesome task of being God's representatives, His deputies. We take the place of God on earth. Kenneth Cragg puts it in this memorable way: "We are here as Master of the earth and as servants of Allah over things because we are under God." Our primary task as human beings is to act on behalf of Allah.

Islam calls our deputyship or vicegerency "Khalifah" (Caliph), from the name given to the successors of the

Prophet. This designation clearly illustrates another uniqueness we have as human beings: We have a "Trust" (Amana) from God (6:165) for which each of us, in our own way, is ultimately responsible.

The Quran constantly reminds Muslims that Allah owns the world and is Master of the universe. "Do you not see that God has subjected to your [use] all things in the heavens and in earth and made His bounties flow to you in exceeding measure, [both] seen and unseen." (31:20) People are expected to be careful managers and stewards of what Allah possesses. In the process of fulfilling our Trusteeship, we may improve or change the creation when our God-given reason deems it advisable. Forgetfulness of our servant role perverts our intelligence and thus our ability to be responsible deputies.

Managers and trustees often forget the stewardship of property entrusted to them and act as if they are owners of it. Such a violation of Trust verges on idolatry and is an affront to Allah. The fulfillment of this Trust is true Islam. It is the willingness to carry out Allah's mission to sustain a healthy environment and a just social order.

Ethics: Principles and Applications

Since Islam is a prophetic religion, it is unavoidably an ethical religion. It is deeply concerned about what happens in this world and how human beings treat each other. Two fundamental relationships—one with God and one with our neighbor—illustrate the inherent connection between ethics and Tawhid (unity of God). Nothing is more central to the Quran than the interrelationship of belief in God and the ethical life. Creed and deed for Islam are like viewing the two sides of an unstamped metallic disc: you don't know which side is which.

This unity is more clearly stated in Sura 2:177. It deserves to be quoted in its entirety:

> Righteousness does not consist in whether you face towards the east or the west. The righteous man is he who believes in Allah and the Last Day, in the Angels and the Scriptures and the prophets, who for the love of Allah gives his wealth to his kinfolk, to the orphan, to the needy, to the wayfarer and to the beggars, and for the redemption of captives; who attends to his prayers and pays the alms-tax, who is true to his promises and steadfast in trial and adversity and

in times of war. Such are the true believers; such are
the God-fearing.

So simply saying you are a Muslim is not enough; perfect
participation in the ritual life of the umma is insufficient. In
both the Quran and the Hadith, the test of religious profession is sensitivity to the neighbor. One of Muhammad's
sayings summarizes it well: "Do you love your Creator?
Love your fellow creature first." This Islamic emphasis is
very similar to the message of the New Testament. One of
John's letters says, "If we say we love God and hate our
neighbor, we are liars." (I John: 4:20)

Because of Islam's stress on submission to God, moral prescriptions and injunctions found in the Quran are taken with
utmost seriousness. The roots of Islamic morality are not
found in philosophical and speculative ethical systems, but
in the will of God. If God says that deeds are what determine our destiny, then Muslims concentrate on doing good
works.

This is not thoughtless adherence to Allah or a lifeless legal-
ism. First of all, Muslims are happy about the specificity of
ethical guidelines in their tradition. They are seen as buoy
markers to warn them of dangerous situations or as banks
which keep the river of moral life flowing as smoothly as
possible. Second, generosity to others, doing the will of
God, and otherwise behaving in an ethical manner, is a
grateful response to the mercy and compassion of Allah. The
Prophet said, "He who is not thankful to his fellow man is

not thankful to Allah." In this sense, Islam is consistent with Judaism and Christianity, which stress gratitude as the authentic source of ethical living.

Some Specific Guidelines

THE TEN COMMANDMENTS

The Quran has its own version of the Ten Commandments in Sura 17:23-40. It is easy to detect the similarity between this list and the one found in Exodus 20.

> Serve no other gods but Allah, lest you incur disgrace and ruin.

> And that you be kind to your parents. If either of them attain old age in your dwelling, show them no sign of impatience, nor rebuke them; but speak to them kind words. Treat them with humility and tenderness and say "Lord, be merciful to them. They nursed me when I was an infant." [This commandment stresses, as does the Jewish version, the crucial place of family in Islamic culture.]

> You shall not commit adultery, for it is foul and indecent.

> You shall not kill any man whom Allah has forbidden you to kill, except for just cause.

> Give full measure when you measure and weigh with even scales.

> Do not follow what you do not know. Man's eyes, ears, and heart—each of his senses will be closely questioned.

Sura 4:32 contains the prohibition of coveting:

> And in no way covet those things in which God has bestowed His gifts more freely on some of you than on others.

The Hadith has a version of the Golden Rule:

> No man is a true believer unless he desires for his brother that which he desires for himself.

Islam rejects some of the "too idealistic for literal acceptance" teachings of Jesus, such as non-resistance to evil (Matthew 5:39-41). Muslim interpreters see this as an extreme reaction to the lex talionis, or "eye for an eye" method of ethical response. Turning the other cheek is not a healthy moral guideline in the presence of tyrants and oppression. It only encourages them to continue their injustice and exploitation, argue Islamic jurists.

Evil must be confronted with any effective means, including violence. Of course, it is expected that we begin with the nonviolence of kindness and mercy, but if that doesn't work, a punishment or response proportionate to the crime is dealt the evildoer. There are several Quranic verses to support this principle: "Nor can goodness and evil be equal. Resist evil with what is good." (41:34) "The recompense of an injury is an injury equal thereto in degree." (42:40)

Western newspapers are fascinated with expressions of retaliatory ethics. It is news because of its rarity; Saudi Arabia and perhaps Pakistan are the only countries where it is strictly practiced. Here is how the Quran reads: "As to the thief, male or female, cut off his or her hands. A punishment by way of example, from God, for their crime." (5:41)

Muslim commentaries of this text, Yusuf Ali's among them, suggest that in most cases, especially those involving petty theft, the teaching is suspended and in more severe cases Islamic jurists help the courts determine the various causes, conditions, and consequences of the theft. As a result, the punishment prescribed seldom happens. A more inclusive retaliatory passage is found in 5:48: "We ordained therein for them: 'Life for life, eye for eye, nose for nose, ear for ear, tooth for tooth and wounds, equal for equal.' But if anyone remits the retaliation by way of charity, it is an act of atonement for himself!" Virtually the same wording is found in Exodus 21:23 and Leviticus 24:18-21. What is strikingly different in the Quranic version is the qualification of mercy, earlier found in the teaching of Jesus in the Sermon on the Mount. Christians might want to remember that in the first century crucifixion was the punishment for thieves. (Matthew 27:38)

WHAT IS HALAL (PERMITTED)
AND WHAT IS HARAM (PROHIBITED

A great deal of what Muslims do is determined by the norms set by these two important concepts, Halal and Haram. Halal, what is allowed, defines for Muslims what is pure and safe; Haram, what is forbidden, points to the impure and the harmful. Both of these standards are found in the Quran and to substitute one for the other is tantamount to Shirk, or idolatry.

Here is a sample list of what is acceptable and forbidden behavior.

Permitted

1. *Wealth*. Muslims view poverty as the work of the Devil. Allah expects us to work hard and amass as much wealth as possible. "The Evil One threatens you with poverty and bids you to unseemly conduct. God presents you His forgiveness and bounty." (2:268) While wealth is seen in a positive light, it is meant to be shared with the less fortunate. "Woe betide every fault-finding, back-slider, who collects wealth and counts it. He thinks his wealth will bestow eternal life upon him." (104:1-3) Money is not to be worshiped or hoarded; miserly people find themselves in the fires of Hell.

An important caveat for Islam is that our wealth should be earned; gambling, cheating, and taking of interest are prohibited precisely because the money which results is unearned and involves no risk on our part. Furthermore, usury exploits people's need for money. International economic transactions, however, make compliance with the ban on interest difficult. Egypt financed the Aswan Dam with a token 2% rate from the Soviet Union.

2. *Abortion* is acceptable until the stage of viability or ensoulment. This is considered about the fourth month of pregnancy for Islam.

3. *Birth Control* is acceptable with the understanding that marriage was designed to produce children.

4. *Divorce* is available for either spouse within framework of Shariah law. Although it is an allowable option, it is not a favored one. The Prophet said, "In the sight of Allah, the most odious of all things permitted is divorce."

5. *Inter-religious Marriage* is permitted for the husband only.

6. *Capital Punishment.* The Quran is clear: "Do not take a life which Allah has made sacred except in the course of justice." (6:151) After the due process set forth in the Shariah and a fair trial, a judge may sentence a person to death. The execution should be carried out by proper authorities. There are three crimes which Allah says require the death penalty:[13]

   a. When someone unjustly murders. Here the law of retaliation is in full effect.

b. The committing of adultery with someone else's wife. Four credible eyewitnesses are needed and they must be willing to testify in court. Either the husband or wife can be charged with this crime.

c. Apostasy from Islam. If, after becoming a Muslim, you act in such a way as to defame Islam and threaten the integrity of the faith, you can be subject to execution. In Islamic countries, apostasy is sometimes identified with treason against the state. In any case, embarrassing Islam, holding it up to ridicule, and being blasphemous may bring the charge of capital punishment.

Prohibited

1. *Slavery*. While it was taken for granted in much of the ancient world, including Biblical times and during the time of Muhammad's revelations, slaves were relatively well cared for, thought of as members of the household, and not the chattel we have come to associate with some modern forms of slavery. Muhammad taught it to be meritorious to free slaves and Abu Bakr redeemed many who became Muslims. It is rarely found in Muslim countries today and is officially prohibited.

2. *Changing of Adopted Child's Name*. Islam requires that all children, including adopted ones, retain the name of the biological father. For the same reason, artificial insemination is not permitted.

3. *Lust* is on a continuum with adultery and other illicit sexual acts. The Quran says we should "lower our gazes" in the presence of the opposite sex. (24:30-31) This does not mean closing our eyes or lowering our head, but as Yusuf al-Qaradawi says, it means "to avert one's gaze from the faces of the passers-by and not to caress the attractive features of the members of the opposite sex with one's eyes." Muhammad is supposed to have told his cousin Ali, the fourth Caliph, "Ali, do not let a second look follow the first. The first look is allowed to you but not the second." (16)

4. *Perverted Sexual Acts.* These include homosexual activity as well as any form of unnatural heterosexual genital expression.

5. *Statues in the House.* This practice is thought to be a form of idol worship and a deterrent to the presence of angels.

6. *Immodest Attire for Women.* "[Women] should draw their veils over their bosoms and not display their beauty except to their husbands" and other close male relatives. (24:31) This dictum was the Quran's reaction to partially clothed, often topless women in pre–Islamic Arabia.

7. *Suicide.* The taking of one's life is as serious as murder.

8. *All pork, and meat from other animals that are improperly slaughtered in the names of other than Allah.*

9. *Alcohol and Gambling.* They are the "gateways " to sin and hinder one from the "remembrance of God." (5:94)

Islam operates under the rule that whatever is not prohibited is permitted. It also is not absolute about all forbidden activity. The ban on pork, for example, is lifted if no other food is available. The specificity of what is Haram helps the average Muslim to make decisions and to pattern his or her life in a way that is socially productive and pleasing to Allah.

Five Pillars of Islam

Islam prescribes guidance for all of life—family life, individual behavior, business transactions, social relations, how to dress, and what to eat. It is natural, then, to find prescriptions for religious obligations and practice. Much of the latter centers on the five pillars or duties of Islam. They are distinguishing marks of a Muslim and practiced by all Muslims of whatever sect everywhere in the world. You could say that Islam is a house built on the rock of submission and supported by these five pillars: Witness, Prayer, Fasting, Almsgiving, and Pilgrimage.

Though all five pillars are generally seen as a unit, and a believer must do all five, one pillar, the Shahadah, stands in the middle. It is the pillar around which all the rest revolve.

Witness to the Faith (Shahadah)

The first pillar is a profession: "There is no God but God, and Muhammad is the Prophet of God." There is nothing more important than this testimony; it is sufficient for conversion and makes a Muslim a Muslim.

So it is chronologically first because it is foundational and all else—the rest of the pillars, ethics, the entire Muslim's life—depends on this declaration of faith. This affirmation constitutes acceptance of the whole message of Islam. Shahadah is a capsule version of the Fatiha which is an abbreviation of the Quran. There are five main elements in Islam's faith (Iman) which is subsumed under the Shahadah:

1. Belief in one God—who alone is worthy of worship;

2. Belief in angels—spiritual beings who do the will of God;

3. Belief in sacred books—including Torah (Taurah) and Gospel (Injil), all inspired by God;

4. Belief in the Prophets—as examples to follow and as spokesmen of God: Noah, Abraham, Moses, and Jesus, primary among others; and

5. Belief in the Day of Judgment and Resurrection.

These words of the Shahadah are said fourteen times a day if a Muslim does all his daily prayers. It is heard at every significant occasion from birth to death and at countless times in between. The Muslim's goal is to be able to make this witness perfectly.

The Shahadah has a negative aspect: "There is no God but God." It clears away any potentially idolatrous debris so the

Muslims can focus on God alone and thus develop an authentic spirituality. There is also a positive dimension to the Shahadah: "And Muhammad is the Prophet of God." By this affirmation, we look to an historical example for the guidance of an ethical life. So the Witness unites the vertical and the horizontal, the spiritual and the ethical. Muhammad said: "I have brought to the world nothing more important than this."

Prayer (Salah)

Probably the visual image most non-Muslims have of Islam is rows of men in a mosque or in a large outdoor space, rhythmically bowing and prostrating in unison. This is Salat, which really means worship, of which prayer is an essential ingredient. This worshipful prayer is pure devotion; it is unconditional praise of God where nothing is asked for, nothing is sought but God alone.

There are two specific words for prayer: _dua,_ which refers to petitions and supplications; and _dhikr,_ the word for "remembrance" used by the Sufis in mystical meditation. These prayers may be spontaneous, unrehearsed, and uttered at any time.

Salat, however, is a prescribed liturgy which includes bodily movement, saying of prayers in Arabic, and recitation of the Quran, all of which are preceded by ritual ablution. Five times a day, at dawn, noon, mid-afternoon, sunset, and at night, the muezzin (_Muadhdhin_—one who calls, a public crier) chants the call to prayer. And then, individually, but preferably with a congregation in the mosque, Muslims gather for Salat. If a mosque is unavailable, a prayer rug may serve as a "mosque." Each rug will have a point in its design to orient the prayer to Mecca. In the absence of a prayer rug, a Muslim can pray any place that is clean. The Prophet said, "The entire earth has been made a masjid (mosque) for me."

A translation of the Call to Prayer is:

God is most great. God is most great.
God is most great. God is most great.
I testify that there is no god except God.
I testify that there is no god except God.
I testify that Muhammad is the messenger of God.
I testify that Muhammad is the messenger of God.
Come to prayer! Come to prayer!
Come to success (in this life and
the Hereafter)! Come to success!
God is most great. God is most great.
There is no god except God.

Before Salat begins, ceremonial bathing occurs at a fountain in the forecourt of the mosque. Without this ritual washing, a symbolic restoration of the believer to original purity and balance, the Salat is not valid. One "bathes one's hands, mouth, nostrils, ears, face, neck, head, one's arms to the elbow, and feet to the ankle. The use of sand is permitted if there is no access to water. The Shahadah is recited throughout the ablutions.

Salat consists of a number of Rakat, or units of prayer. A Rakah (singular) includes certain bodily movements with accompanying words of prayer and scripture. These are learned by all Muslims at the age of seven and performed in the same manner the world over. This is how a Rakah progresses:

1. Standing facing qibla with hands raised to ears, reciting (Takbir)—Allahu Akbar or God is greatest;

2. Still standing, folding hands in front of your waist, reciting the Fatiha;

3. Bowing from the hips with hands on knees, reciting another Takbir;

4. Resuming standing position, followed by prostration (a bodily symbol of our humility and submission to the will of God);

5. Raising your body to a sitting position (a form of kneeling), saying Takbir;

6. From this position, performing another prostration, repeating Takbir; and

7. Then sitting for silent prayers, blessing God, turning your face from side to side to acknowledge your neighbors in Salam.

One cycle of the varous bodily positions to perform Salat is depicted in the Rakat that follows. [Photos by Mary D. Zepp]

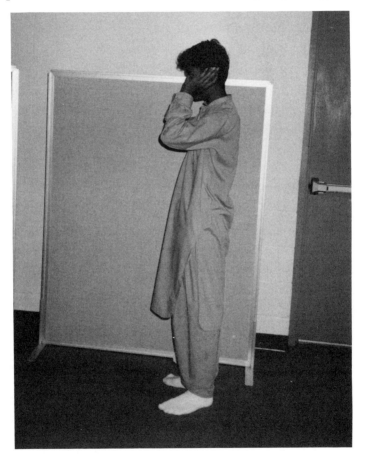

1. Hands are raised to say "Allahu Akbar"

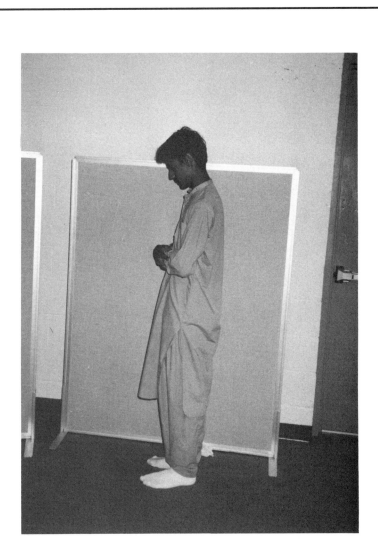

2. The standing position to recite the Fatiha

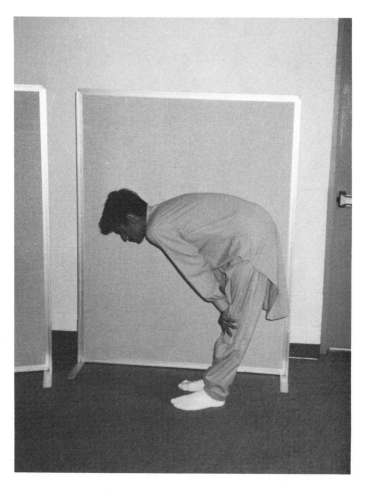

3. One bows to repeat three times:
"Glory be to God the Mighty"

4. While prostrating, one says:
"Glory to My Lord the Most High"

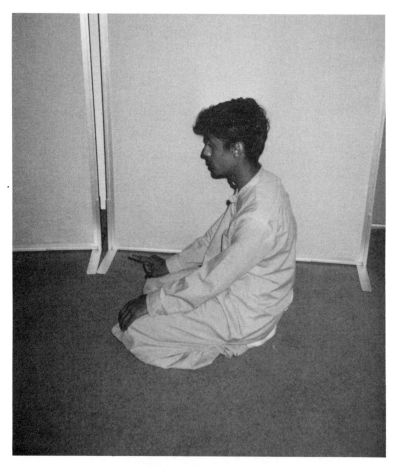

*5. Seated with one finger extended
to symbolize the Unity of Allah*

A prayer (Salat) consists of two to four units. Dawn salat has two; at evening there are three, and the rest of the prayer times have four each, with a total of seventeen units per day. The basic physical positions are standing, bowing, sitting (kneeling), and prostration.

As we have mentioned, the Quran is always used during prayer. Any Sura or part of a Sura may be recited, depending on the individual's preference for verses. But some of the most used passages are the Fatiha, Sura 112 (The Oneness of God), 114 (Humankind), 2:255 (the famous "Throne Verse") 24:35 (Light), and 59:22-24 (some wonderful names of God).

These daily acts of worship have the effect of sanctifying the whole day. They punctuate the daily routine with five remembrances of God which hopefully substitute a consciousness of God for care and anxiety.

The weekly noonday prayers on Fridays are a communal Salat. They are directed by an Imam who leads rows of men in prayer. Women may join men, but must stand in separate lines. More typically, women perform their acts of worship at home.

The reader may have noticed no reference to intercessory prayer. The Quran does not mention prayers of intercession because God does not require from any person what is beyond his or her power (2:233). One of the most quoted verses of the Quran is: "God's mercy comprehends everything" (7:156), including our asking help for others. God knows our needs and in His mercy will act accordingly. In practice, at the end of the formal prayer sequence, the worshiper is free to sit quietly in personal and informal prayer (dua) and petition, praise, thank or even beg from God. Salat is a symbol of just how important prayer is for Islam.

Fasting (Sawm)

Prayer and fasting, the second and third pillars, are disciplines found in every religion and Islam makes a significant place for both of them in the lives of Muslims. Fasting is primarily reserved for the month of Ramadan. Even the most assimilated Muslim will observe this fast for the ninth month of the lunar year. In Sura 2:183-185, the Quran spells out the rationale for fasting and what is required of the Muslim during this time of self-purification.

The month of Ramadan was chosen for the annual period of personal spiritual renewal because it was in the last ten days of Ramadan that Muhammad experienced his "Night of Power" and first received revelations from Allah which were to become the Quran.

Ramadan punctuates the year with a holy time in much the same way prayer time sanctifies each day.

There are two sides to Ramadan—one is negative (self-denial) and the other is positive (appreciation for the simplest gifts of Allah—food and drink and charity for the neighbor).

From sunrise to sunset for the entire twenty-nine to thirty days of the month one is to fast from food, drink (including water), gambling, sexual activity, and all sensuous pleasures (including music). One also attempts a fast from evil thoughts and desires. Total abstinence reminds the Muslim that his or her life is one of sacrifice and a life finally dependent on God.

Since the calendar is a lunar one, the ninth month of Ramadan comes at different times during the year. When it falls in winter and the days are shorter, the sacrifice is less. But one's spiritual commitment is tested when one has to fast on long summer days. Furthermore, Ramadan helps the Muslims appreciate, in a very special way, the significance of the seasons and the wondrous thing that is the universe created by Allah.

If the fast adversely affects one's health, that person is exempted. Pregnant, nursing, and menstruating women are exempted and may compensate for their lost days during other times in the year.

Ramadan is, as someone has said, "a yearly training program," a time of spiritual enrichment and discipline to re-empower the Muslim for another year of Islam. It is a time when the spiritual values of love, honesty, devotion, generosity, and social concern are deepened.

Ramadan is not only a time of renunciation and self-denial. It is also a joyful month. When the daily fast is broken at sunset, there is a light meal (*iftar*—break-fast) and the streets of the town or city are full of people in a festive mood. About two hours before sunrise Muslims have an early morning meal to prepare themselves for another day of fasting.

Beyond the ascetic aspect of Ramadan, there are positive goals. One is to listen to or recite the entire Quran during the month. This is made easier for the average person by having the Quran divided into thirty equal portions. Another positive goal is that fasting helps the Muslim identify with the needs of the "have-nots." So each day, a Muslim is expected to do a good deed and contribute to a charitable cause.

At the end of Ramadan, there is a day of celebrating (*Eid Al-Fitr*—Feast of the Breaking of the Fast). It is a grand time for family reunions and gift giving, and a holiday that children, in particular, enjoy.

Almsgiving (Zakat)

This is another example of Islam's concern for the poor. Zakat, the fourth pillar, is a kind of social security system and organized welfare program which helps a Muslim society share its wealth and maintain an equitable society.

Zakat is a tax of two-and-one-half percent of one's annual savings—what remains after personal and business expenses. This tax is beyond what one might donate to charity and the many different state taxes which become a part of a public fund to be used for the general welfare and a number of human services.

Almsgiving is an act of worship, very much like prayer and fasting, and is earmarked for the poor, needy, disabled, and other deprived people. It represents the universal religious impulse in people to share their wealth with those who are less fortunate. Zakat literally means "purification"; it purifies the giver and what is given.

A Muslim leader in early Islam observed how prayer, fasting, and almsgiving were related: "Prayer carries us halfway to God; fasting brings us to the door of His praises; almsgiving procures for us admission."

Pilgrimage (Hajj)*

This last pillar is the crowning experience of a Muslim's life and moves his or her heart as nothing else. Once in a lifetime, if health and material means permit, a Muslim is expected to make a religious journey to Mecca. The pilgrimage usually involves a good deal of personal sacrifice—time, effort, and perhaps a life's savings. It is imperative that money for the pilgrimage be earned by the pilgrim. A Hajj is invalid if one has to go in debt to make the trip.

But for the Muslim, the journey to and presence in Mecca is the ultimate act of worship. It is an opportunity to re-enact the founding of Islam and renew links with Abraham, Ha-

*Much of the following is gleaned from Ismail and Lois L. Faruqi's *A Cultural Atlas of Islam* and a booklet entitled *Pilgrimage* distributed by Muslim Students Association of U.S. and Canada, 1974.

gar, Ishmael, and of course, Muhammad. Hajj is a return to origins, to roots, to the prestige of the beginnings.

Hajj also allows the participant to experience the egalitarian nature and radical unity of Islam. Muslims from around the world—all classes, colors, nationalities, and races—are there in the same dress, performing the same rituals. There is no rank or privilege in this holy place because we are without rank before Allah. The pilgrimage is also a foretaste of the Day of Judgment, especially as the pilgrims stand in pious devotion on the plain of Arafat near the Mount of Mercy.

Hajj has the meaning of "to set out for a definite purpose" or "to visit a revered place." The rationale for pilgrimage and certain prescribed activities surrounding it are found in Suras 2:196-203 and 5:98-100.

About sixty days after the end of Ramadan, the month of pilgrimage (Dhu al-Hijja) begins. During the first ten days of this twelfth month of the year, around two million Muslims will travel to Mecca. If one cannot make the trip, and the majority of Muslims do not perform Hajj, a substitute is prescribed. It is the feast of *Id al-Adha* (Feast of Sacrifice) which is performed on the tenth day of the month at home to coincide with the same feast the pilgrims are enjoying in Mecca. The feast is a one-day ceremony for prayer and, if the family or person can afford it, the sacrifice of an animal. This sacrifice remembers the ram provided Abraham by the angel and consequently celebrates Ishmael's freedom. A portion of this sacrificial meal is given to the poor.

KAABA

The "holy of holies" for Islam is a cube-shaped building in the middle of the courtyard of the Grand Mosque in Mecca. In religious studies we call this sort of place an *"axis mundi."* This "center of the world" unifies all reality for Islam and around this axis, all Muslims turn. The qibla in every mosque directs daily prayer toward the Kaaba.

It has a rich and venerable history. Tradition states that it is the first structure built by a monotheist for the worship of one God.

Some Muslims claim it was first built by Adam, but a stronger tradition has Abraham and Ishmael constructing the first Kaaba about 2000 years BCE (2:125). Obviously, a pilgrimage to Mecca to visit the Kaaba preceded Islam and Muhammad. But by Muhammad's time, this center of worship had deteriorated from a shrine for Abrahamic monotheism to a place containing 360 idols.

The present Kaaba is about 40 feet long, 33 feet wide, and 50 feet high. It is covered with a black cloth with verses from the Quran embroidered on it in gold thread. The four corners of the Kaaba coincide with the four cardinal points of the compass. This sacred precinct, including the city of Mecca, is haram; it is forbidden territory for non-Muslims.

Of particular interest is the Black Stone set in the eastern corner of the Kaaba. This stone, about twelve inches in diameter, which a Hadith of Muhammad says came from heaven, is a relic from the original Kaaba. It becomes the focal point of the pilgrims as they walk around the Kaaba. They begin their circular procession from the location of the Black Stone and as each pilgrim passes the Stone, it is either touched, kissed, or otherwise acknowledged.

The Kaaba: A cube-shaped building in the middle of the courtyard of The Grand Mosque in Mecca. It is believed to be the first monument erected to a monotheistic deity and is the holiest of shrines for Islam. [A Saudi Aramco Photo]

THE PILGRIM RITUAL

This is what the pilgrim does when he or she makes the Pilgrimage to Mecca.

1. Preparation. First of all, one is expected to achieve a stage of purity and consecration before Hajj begins. This is symbolized in several ways: a) solemnly declaring an intention to do Hajj, b) taking a ritual bath, and c) (some distance from Mecca) changing from your ordinary clothes to your pilgrim dress (ihram) which consists of pieces of white unsewn cotton garments (women wear one piece of unsewn cloth over their ordinary clothes). In this state of restriction, one cannot cut one's hair, nails, wear perfume, hunt, argue or have sexual relations.

Ihram signifies a state of peace, self-abasement, and submission to God. The pilgrim is now ready for the sacred journey to the holy city. After arriving in Mecca, the pilgrim's ritual activity will take about three days.

First Day

2. "Going Around the Kaaba" (Tawaf). The Kaaba is circumambulated seven times in counterclockwise direction beginning at the eastern corner where the Black Stone is located. I have been told that pilgrims at this moment are deeply in earnest, saying prayers, and reciting the Quran. It is for them a time of solemn intimacy with God.

3. "Hastening" (Saai). After circling the Kaaba, the pilgrim slowly runs seven* times between Safa and Marwa, two small hills in Mecca. This activity commemorates Hagar's frantic search for water to assuage Ishmael's thirst. While she was running around these hills, Ishmael made a hole in the sand with his heel. From this hole sprang a well of water to save his life. This well, called Zamzam, exists to this day and pilgrims make a point to drink from this Holy Well as part of their time in Mecca.

These hills are now located at each end of the northwest wall of the huge mosque which surrounds the Kaaba.

4. After Saai, the pilgrim travels thirteen miles away to one end of the plain of Arafat near the Mount of Mercy where Muhammad delivered his last sermon. Here the pilgrim "stands" in reverent devotion from about noon to sunset. Prayers said at this time at Arafat are particularly efficacious. Muhammad said of them: "The best of prayers is the prayer of the day of Arafat." On the return trip to Mecca one usually stops at Muzdalifa (about five miles from Arafat) to spend the night. From here it is only three miles to a small town called Mina for another important ritual.

---

*Seven is considered a holy number in Biblical tradition. It represents perfection, wholeness, and completeness. Cf. Seventh Heaven, Seventh Day.

Second Day

5. *Mina*. This is where Muslims believe Ishmael's sacrifice was to have taken place. In Mina are three stone pillars of varying size; these monoliths represent the three places Satan tempted Ishmael to rebel against his father's willingness to obey God. Ishmael rebuked the Devil by throwing stones at him each time a temptation occurred. Pilgrims re-enact this resistance to Satan by throwing seven pebbles at each of the three pillars, symbolizing their resolution to resist temptation. "Allah is greatest" is said each time a pebble is thrown.

After casting their stones, pilgrims offer an animal sacrifice. This is not an act of atonement, but a joyful remembrance of Abraham's sacrifice of a ram instead of his son. Ishmael's patience and perseverance and Abraham's submission to God are celebrated by the sacrifice. Having ritually dealt with the Devil, the pilgrims return to Mecca.

Third Day

6. After their return to Mecca, they go around the Kaaba again seven times and jog seven more times between Safa and Marwa. Once these final steps are completed, pilgrims de-sacralize themselves by clipping their hair and replacing their pilgrim's garments with ordinary clothes. Now they are spiritually reborn; they are Hajji (men) or Hajjah (women)—they have made the pilgrimage and been blessed.

There is a Lesser Pilgrimage (Umrah) in which Muslims go to Mecca at any time of the year to perform an abbreviated Hajj. They wear pilgrim's clothes, circle the Kaaba, and jog between the small hills. This is not a substitute for the Greater Hajj which is a pillar of Islam.

As part of their sacred journey, many pilgrims go to Medina to visit Muhammad's Tomb and the Prophet's Mosque. If possible, they also will visit the "Farthest Mosque" (Al-Aqsa) in Jerusalem to celebrate Muhammad's "Night Journey."

What is JIHAD?

JIHAD is another Arabic word, meaning STRIVING.

Islam teaches Muslims that they must "strive"
or work hard to make their religion real in their
lives and in their societies. This should be done
by JIHAD on four levels:

JIHAD of the TONGUE: speaking about their faith;
JIHAD of the HAND: putting their faith into action
     by good works;
JIHAD of the HEART: making their faith real
     as a spiritual force in their lives;
JIHAD of the SWORD: defending their faith when
     they fear it to be under attack.

From "Questions and Answers About Islam" by David A. Kerr;
used by permission.

Jihad (Striving, Struggle)

The essential meaning of Jihad is the spiritual, psychological, and physical effort we exert to be close to God and thus achieve a just and harmonious society. Jihad literally means "striving" or "struggle" and is shorthand for *Jihad fi Sabeel Allah* (struggle in God's cause). In a sense, every Muslim is a Mujahid, one who strives for God and justice. So central is this practice of Islam that from the beginning some Muslims have called Jihad a "missing imperative" or "neglected duty," that is, a "sixth pillar."

Al-Ghazali captured the essence of Jihad when he said: "The real Jihad is the warfare against the passions." Dr. Ibrahim Abu-Rabi calls Jihad "the execution of effort against evil in the self and every manifestation of evil in society." In a way, Jihad is the Muslim's purest sacrifice: to struggle to live a perfect life and completely submit to God.

Another form of Jihad is the striving to translate the Word of God into action. If one has experienced God and received Guidance from the Quran, one struggles to apply that Guidance in daily life. So the larger, more prevalent meaning of Jihad is the spiritual struggle of the soul. In this case, Jihad is always present for the believer whether there is an external enemy or not. We should never reduce Jihad to violence.

A third level of Jihad is popularly known as "holy war." The classic passage is found in 2:190: "Fight for the sake of Allah those that fight against you, but do not attack them first. Allah does not love aggressors."

It is crucial to note here that what is condoned is defensive warfare; Islam cannot justify aggressive war. Muhammad and the Tradition are also against killing non-combatants, torturing of prisoners, the destruction of crops, animals, and homes.[14]

It is unfortunate that Islam has been stereotyped as the "religion of the sword" or that Islam was "spread by the sword." The historical reality is that the expansion of Islam was usually by persuasion and not by military power. In any case, Islam cannot be forced on anyone; if profession of the Shahadah is forced on someone, it is not true Islam. "There is no constraint in religion," says the Quran. F. Rahman said, "what was spread by the sword was not the religion of Islam, but the political domain of Islam so that Islam could work to produce the order on the earth that the Quran seeks."[15]

The several occasions which would prompt the Muslim to apply the Jihad of the sword are: (1) to defend oneself, family, country, and religion (4:75), (2) to defend fellow Muslims who are helpless and oppressed (8:72), and (3) to secure religious freedom (a reflection of number 1 above).

Since the defense of Islam is fighting in the name of God, warfare is a sacred duty. If one is killed in a Jihad, he is a martyr (Shahid) according to the Quran: "As for those who are slain in the cause of Allah, He will not allow their works to perish. He will vouchsafe them guidance and ennoble their state; He will admit them to the Paradise He has made known to them." (47:4-5)

The specific laws which determine a genuine Jihad are very similar to the "just-war theory" in Christianity. Practically speaking, however, a true Jihad is rarely invoked. Certain Muslim factions, in the name of self-interest, will engage in political struggle and call it Jihad, but no individual or group can arbitrarily wage Jihad. Only the state, through its leaders—the Caliph or Imam—can authorize a Holy War.

The Muslim Wedding and Funeral

Before a Muslim man or woman can be married, a dowry must be arranged for the wife and they must sign a marriage contract. This ritual is performed in the presence of an Imam or, if the couple lives in an Islamic nation, before a Judge or an Imam. Two witnesses who are Muslim must be present to help legitimize the marriage.

Marriage is not a sacrament in Islam; it is a social contract to establish a family unit, which in turn benefits the entire Muslim umma.

Signing the marriage contract is absolutely essential to make a man and woman husband and wife. After the contract signing, the couple may have a wedding. The wedding is an occasion when invited guests, including extended family and friends of the bride and groom, gladly join in publicly celebrating the contract entered into by the happy couple. Actually, the wedding is a public announcement of the marriage which has already taken place.

At times, the wedding and the signing of the marriage contract can be united in one event; at other times, depending on the couple, the contract signing may be all that is desired.

The following is a sample marriage contract a Muslim couple
signs and a typical wedding sermon read by an Imam at a
Muslim wedding. They were given to me by Imam M.
Bashar Arafat, Director of the Islamic Society of Baltimore
and are used here with his permission.

Islamic Society of Baltimore, Maryland, Inc.
P.O. Box 7647, Baltimore, Maryland 21207

MARRIAGE CONTRACT

THE BRIDEGROOM:
In the Name of Allah, Most Gracious, Most Merciful:
With His Help and Guidance;
With all my trust put in Him;
With my full awareness of responsibility;
And with my free choice and freedom of will,
I, _____, solemnly propose to marry Miss
_____, and take her as my wife, in accor-
dance with the teachings of the Qur'an, and the Sunnah of
our Prophet Muhammad ibn Abdullah (P.B.U.H.).
I declare this solemn proposal before the present witnesses,
praying Almighty Allah to be my witness;
Allah is the best of all witnesses.

THE BRIDE
In the Name of Allah, Most Gracious, Most Merciful:
With His Help and Guidance;
With all my trust put in Him;
With my full awareness of responsibility;
And with my free choice and freedom of will;
I, _____, accept your solemn proposal to take
me as your wife in accordance with the teachings and laws of the
Qur'an and the Sunnah of the Prophet Muhammad (P.B.U.H.).
I make this declaration before the present witnesses, praying to
Almighty Allah to be my witness;
Allah is the best of all witnesses.

Bismillah hir Rahman nir Rahim

MARRIAGE SERMON

A. All praise is due to Allah; we thank and glorify Him; and beseech Him for help; and we ask for His forgiveness and protection; and we seek refuge in Allah from the temptations of our self and from the evil of our deeds:

Whomsoever Allah guides, there is none who can lead him astray, and whomsoever Allah leaves in error there is none to guide him.

We bear witness that there is none worthy of worship except Allah, He is One, No associate has He:

And we bear witness that Muhammad is His servant and His Messenger.

B. I seek refuge in Allah from Satan the outcast.

Allah has said in the Quran:

O you who believe, Keep your duty to Allah as it ought to be kept, and do not die unless you are Muslims. (3:101)

O people, Keep your duty to your Lord, Who created you from a single being and of the same created its mate, and spread from these two many men and women.

And keep your duty to Allah, By Whom you demand one of another your rights and to the time of relationship.

Surely Allah is ever watcher over you. (4:1)

O you who believe, keep your duty to Allah and speak straight words: He will put your deeds into a right state for you, and forgive you your sins;

And whoever obeys Allah and His Messenger he indeed achieves a mighty success.

C. Prophet Muhammad (peace be unto him) has said: "The world and all things in it are valuable; but the most valuable thing in the world is a virtuous woman."

"Marriage is a tradition of mine; whosoever turns his face away from my tradition does not belong to me."

"When a person marries he completes half of his faith; let him take awe in Allah concerning the other half."

D. And whosoever obeys Allah and His Messenger surely he is guided; and whosoever disobeys them he does not harm anyone but himself, and he does not harm Allah a bit.

And we beseech Allah to make us among those who obey Him and we obey His Messenger, and follow His pleasure and keep themselves away from His wrath; Surely we are from Him and for Him.

O Allah, Bless our dear leader Muhammad, the Prophet, the Unlettered one, and his followers and his companions and his wives and his descendants and his family and salute them all with a worthy salutation.

To this may be added a prayer for the welfare and prosperity of the couple. The words of a prayer as reported in Hadith are:

May Allah shower His Blessings on you and may He bless you and unite you two in goodness.

THE MUSLIM FUNERAL

The dying Muslim will have the Shahadah on his or her lips. After death, the body will be buried quickly, hopefully before sundown on the day of death. Because of its emphasis on the Resurrection of the body, Islam, along with orthodox Jews and many Christians, do not allow cremation.

Mourners usually say prayers (*dua*) for the dead at any time in the mosque and always after the stated daily prayers.

As the deceased is carried to the cemetery, the Shahadah is chanted. The body is buried with the right side facing Mecca. Muslims are buried in traditional funeral wrappings rather than a coffin, although there is no prohibition against the latter. The funeral wrapping is a seamless white shroud, hopefully a piece of cloth dipped in the well of Zamzam during the Hajj.

THE FUNERAL RITES*

Washing of the Dead

1. The clothing of the dead is removed. The genitals are to be covered.

2. The body will be abluted (like ablution before regular prayer, except that the arms will not be washed and the mouth and nose will not be rinsed with water). The head will be washed with water and soap (it is not sufficient to wipe the head as in the regular ablution).

3. Water will be poured over the body three times. The first time, the body will be placed on the left side to allow water to be poured on the right side. The second time is the contrary. Then the body will be placed in a sitting position leaning on the breast of the washer, and the abdomen will be gently wiped. The last time, the whole body will be washed with water and a detergent-like soap.

4. A man washes a man, and a woman washes a woman. A woman may wash her husband, and a man or woman may wash young boys and girls.

Shrouding

1. The man is to be shrouded in three layers. The first sheet extends from the neck to above the feet. The second extends from the head to the feet. The third is a larger cover than the latter—it exceeds the head and feet, and will be tied above the head and below the feet.

---

*These rites surrounding the death and burial of a Muslim have been furnished by The Islamic Center of Washington, D.C.

2. The woman is to be shrouded in five layers. The
first is something like a shirt or chemise in a very simple form. The second is a short veil to be put on the
head and face loosely. The third is a sheet of cloth
to be enclosed from the head to the feet. The fourth
is a sheet of cloth to be fastened around the abdomen
and breast. The fifth is a large cover to hide the entire
body.

3. In the case of a young girl, it is sufficient to use the
first and the last only.

The Prayer

1. The Imam, who is anyone from among the Muslim
community, will place the dead before him in the direction of "Qibla" (the direction of Mecca). He will stand,
with the other Muslims present standing behind him
doing as he does. The Imam is preferable to be a leader
in the Muslim community or a relative of the dead.

2. The Imam and the followers must declare an intention privately before they begin the prayers for the dead.

3. The Imam will make Takbirah (that is to say: Allahu
Akbar), and he will read Al-Fatiha (the opening chapter
of the Holy Quran).

4. He will then make the second Takbirah and will recite the second part of At-Tashahhud (from Allahumma
salli 'ala Sayyidina Mohammad, to: Innaka Hamidun
Majid).

5. He will make the third Takbirah and ask the Lord's
mercy for the dead and for all Muslims by any words
he likes, or preferably by saying as the tradition of the

Prophet says: "Alla-humma-ghfer li-hayyina wa-mayyitina wa-saghirina wa-kabirina wa-dhakarina wa-onthana wa-shahidina wa-ghaibina. Allahumma man ahyaytahu menna fa-ahyihi 'ala-l-Islam. Wa-man tawaffaytahu menna fatawaffahu 'ala-lImam. Allahomma la tahrimna ajrah wala taftinna ba'adah." This means: "O Lord, have mercy on the whole of us, our survivors and our dead, our young and our adult, our male and our female, our present and our absent. O Lord, those whom You cause to survive, keep them on Islam, and those whom You cause to die, make them die on the true faith. O Lord, do not prevent us from the reward we deserve, because of our patience on the loss, and do not let us be misguided after him.
6. The Imam will make the fourth Takbirah and will say: "Allahumma la tahrimna ajrah wala taftinna ba' adah, waghfir lana walah." This means: "O Lord, do not prevent us from the reward we deserve, and do not let us be misguided, after him, and have mercy on us and on him."
7. The Imam will direct his face to the right, saying in a loud voice: "Assalumnu Alaykom." Then, on the left side, saying: "Assalumu Alaykom."

Remark: All of these recitations except the four Takbiras and the Greeting, must be said privately, not in a raised voice.

Divisions in Islam

Sunni and Shiite:
How Will Leadership Be Determined?

Muhammad, while providing so much for Muslim welfare, left the Muslims to determine for themselves how and by whom they would be governed after he was gone. Support was voiced immediately for the friends of Muhammad, Abu Bakr, and for Ali, who was Muhammad's cousin (son of Abu Talib) and son-in-law (husband of Fatima). Ali's supporters were under the impression that the Prophet wanted someone in the family to be the successor, and Abu Bakr's group was just as certain that Muhammad wanted someone who most exemplified the spirit and character of the Prophet.

Ali's group was called Shiites, literally "partisans," or those belonging to the party of Ali. Abu Bakr's contingent was called Sunnis, that is, those who followed the example or custom of the Prophet. So the real difference between Sunnis and Shiites is "Who is qualified to be the leader of the umma?" Should it be one who is related by blood to Muhammad (Ali's position) or should it be one who best exemplifies the life and thought of Muhammad? That difference of opinion persists to this day. What distinguishes Sunnis and Shiites is not that one is conservative and one is liberal or that one interprets Shariah in a certain way. They do not differ in fundamental Islamic belief and practice; indeed, they are nourished by the same sources—Quran and Hadith. The crucial difference lies in the answer to the question: "Who will be our leader?"

A review of the earliest days of Islam will reveal how these divisions unfolded. Abu Bakr, Muhammad's closest ally and father-in-law (father of Aisha, his favorite wife after Khadija), was elected the first Caliph, in spite of resistance from Ali's supporters. A Caliph was a deputy or representative of the Prophet. As a form of political and religious leadership, it lasted in the Sunni tradition until the twentieth century.

Abu Bakr appeared to be a logical choice. He had a long association with the Prophet and had appropriated much of Muhammad's sensitivity, wisdom, and experience. To this was added Abu Bakr's own natural inclination for moderation.

Abu Bakr led the new Muslim community for two years (632-634) and was followed by Umar, who was Caliph from 634 to 644. Umar was known primarily as a military strategist and was responsible for many early victories of the fledgling religion. Most of all, Umar is remembered for his conquest of Persia.

In 644 Umar was followed by Uthman, whose Caliphate lasted until 656. The distinction of his rule was the final editing of the authorized version of the Quran.

After three successful Caliphates of the Sunni tradition, Ali became the fourth Caliph. He also had fine credentials. Besides being related to the Prophet, he accompanied Muhammad to Medina on that famous Hegira. He was also a loyal supporter of Islam's rapidly expanding religious and political empire. Many of Ali's party thought Muhammad actually preferred him as the natural heir to the Prophet's legacy.

In truth, all four of the first caliphs had excellent backgrounds and abilities for leadership. They were all eyewitnesses, early converts, and faithful companions of Muhammad. All four, in general, shared Muhammad's vision of Islam. Because of this, the first four Caliphs were called "Rightly Guided Ones" (Rashidun). They ruled in what might be called "an apostolic era," a normative and standard time by which Muslims of later generations would judge themselves.

A Seventh-Century Sect and an Eighteenth-Century Sect

Kharjites: a seventh-century sect which broke away from both Sunnis and Shiites over the issue of leadership. Kharjites felt that the Caliph should be the most morally worthy person whose appointment remains "in the hands of God" and not a politicized office.

Wahhabis: founded in the late eighteenth-century by Muhammad ibn Abd al-Wahhab (d. 1787). It is a puritanical interpretation of Islam which literally interprets the Quran and is utterly loyal to traditions of Shariah, especially laws regarding women. It is the religious legacy of the Saud dynasty which rules much of the Arabian peninsula and the reason Saudi Arabia is one of the most conservative of Islamic countries.

SUNNI ISLAM

The number of Sunnis in the world is almost the proportion
of Sunnis in the "Rightly Guided Ones." They were 75% of
the first four Caliphs and comprise about 85-90% of today's
Muslim population. They represent the custom (Sunna) of
Muhammad and are mainstream, "standard brand" Muslims.
The Sunni tradition is not known for its special religious
leaders, such as the imams in the Shiite community. They
simply want Islam to preserve the faithful practice of the
Prophet and keep continuity with the tradition of the early
umma.

Two Major Schools of Theology (Kalam) in Sunni Tradition

During the Golden Age of Islam (eighth to thirteenth century
CE), two major theological schools emerged. They give am-
ple evidence that Islam was taken with utmost intellectual
seriousness. Islam could be thought as well as lived!

Their differences lay in matters of emphasis and are not mutually exclusive. Both founders, ibn Ata and al-Ashari, were
sophisticated theologians and their dedication to Islam was
never in doubt.

Al-Ashari's force as a thinker gained the support of the majority of Sunnis. It is a tribute to the school that the
renowned al-Ghazali (1058-1111) became one of its most
articulate advocates. While the school's influence may have

climaxed in the twelfth century, its legacy lives on in much of twentieth-century Islam.

Here are the two schools with their distinguishing characteristics:

MUTAZILITES
Founder: Wasil ibn Ata (d. 749)
Characteristics:
— emphasis on reason as final arbiter in issues of faith
— emphasis on human freedom and responsibility
— critical of predestination as inconsistent with freedom of people
— use of allegorical method in interpreting the Quran
— Quran is eternal, but the words, the meaning conveying the message, were created for seventh-century Islam.
— dominant in Persia during Abbasid Empire

ASHARITES
Founder: Ali ibn Ismail al-Ashari (d. 935)
Characteristics:
— emphasis on revelation as final authority
— retained orthodox Islam theology
— defended predestination as central belief in Islam
— Quran is eternal and the words we have were with God from the beginning.
— dominant today in the Islamic West

Major Schools of Law in Sunni Tradition

These four orthodox schools differ slightly in their legal interpretations and how those interpretations apply to the practical day-to-day life of Muslims, for example, marriage, ritual ablutions, Jihad, political decisions, etc.

Name of School	Founder	Primary Location
Hanifi	Abu Hanifa (d. 767)	Turkey, India, Pakistan, Afghanistan
Maliki	Maliki ibn Anas (d. 795)	West Africa, North Africa
Shafi	Muhammad al-Shafi (d. 820)	Indonesia, Egypt, Philippines, Malaysia, Sri Lanka
Hanbali	Ahmad ibn Hanbal (d. 855)	Saudi Arabia

In spite of the many schools of law and theology, the final authority for Sunni Muslims is the interpretation of the Quran and Hadith by the *ulema*, a group of learned scholars. This is in contrast to the Shiites who rely on their religious leaders, the imams, for definitive guidance.

SHIITE ISLAM

Historical Background

After a five-year Caliphate, Ali was assassinated in 661. His death triggered a bitter controversy over what would be the criterion for succession: the Prophet's example or his blood-line.

Ali wanted his oldest son, Hasan, first grandson of Muhammad, to be the fifth caliph and second Imam. This, indeed, happened; but at the same time, and as an act of defiance, Muawiyah, from the Umayyad tribe of Quraysh, claimed the caliphate for himself.

After a brief reign of only six months, Hasan abdicated in an attempt to preserve the unity of Muslims. Muawiyah then became the sixth caliph. Muawiyah, however, seemed to have little appreciation for Hasan's gesture, and began treating the descendants of the Prophet Muhammad as his political enemies. Finally, Husayn, the younger son of Ali, mounted a rebellion against Muawiyah. This was the decisive rupture between the Sunnis and Shiites. Yazid, who succeeded his father, Muawiyah,* then engaged Husayn in a

---

*Actually, this hereditary succession violated Sunni custom, but the Umayyad dynasty led the Meccan opposition to Muhammad, so whatever they could do to discredit the caliphate was in their self-interest. It is here we see clearly the convergence of the political and the religious in the formation of Shiism.

fierce battle at Karbala in 680. Husayn, less equipped and understaffed, was soundly defeated. His death was viewed by Ali's partisans as a multiple tragedy: personal, family, and national. In short, it became a "sacred" event with Husayn the martyr and Karbala, one of the holiest shrines of Shiite Islam.

Because of Husayn's martyrdom in resisting overwhelming odds and because, after inviting him to Iraq, many Shiites felt they inadequately supported Husayn and thus betrayed him, Shiism sees its origin in a redemptive, purifying sacrifice. A commemoration of this sacrifice is held annually in Karbala with thousands of pilgrims engaged in self-flagellation and breast-beating—some have called it a Shiite passion play. In any case, it is a form of collective suffering to assuage the collective guilt of betraying Husayn.

The sense of being born in suffering energizes this minority and provides a common identity. That same energy fuels much of the political and religious activity in Iran and Iraq today.

The Place of Ali in Shiism

Ali Ibn in Abi Talib was his full name. His father was the uncle who adopted Muhammad as his son, so both the Prophet and Ali belong to the same Hashimite clan and were first cousins.* He was one of the first to accept Muhammad's

---

*The contemporary King Hussein of Jordan traces his lineage to the Prophet's grandson and claims membership in the same Hashimite clan.

call to Islam and was a steadfast companion, brave warrior, and wise leader. Cyril Glassé indicates how revered Ali was by all Muslims: "He is remembered for his piety, nobility, and learning. Besides being courageous, he acted towards his enemies with generosity and magnanimity."[16]

Ali was obviously close to the Prophet. Muhammad called him his "brother" and three times his "heir." Ali and Fatima received a rare marriage blessing in the form of an anointing from Muhammad. Because of the emotional bond and deference shown by Muhammad, it is easy to see why Ali's friends would think he was the natural successor to the Prophet. Ali did evidence some grace by being a consultant to the first three caliphs.

As the first imam, Ali became the model for imams to follow. In retrospect, some Shiites invested him with an un-Islamic significance he never intended. Some extreme sects even thought he had been appointed by Allah and divinely inspired. He was held in such high veneration that some even called him divine and today a group of Shiites add "and Ali is the vicegerent of Allah" to their Shahadah.

Nature of the Imam

For most of Islam, the imam is known as a leader of prayer in Friday services in mosques. It can also be a title of honor for outstanding thinkers, such as founders of legal and theological schools. But for Shiites, in particular, the imam is much more than a worship leader. At certain points in history, a select few imams are singled out by virtue of their sanctity, wisdom, and spiritual power. They become infallible intermediaries between people and God. They are "credited with supernatural knowledge and authority, and with a station of merit, which, as it were, is an extension of, and virtually equal with, that of the Prophet."[17]

In some cases, the imam is elevated to a station higher than the prophet. Why? Because he is dead and the imamate, in its historical struggle, has suffered more than Muhammad. For the most devout of Shiites, to be in the presence of an imam is to be in the presence of Allah. It is much the same feeling a Catholic has in the presence of the Pope. Once this nature of the imamate is understood, you can appreciate the regard Shiites have for their holy men.

Shiite Sects

The largest and most recognized Shiite sect is the Twelvers. Its history is rooted in the reverence elicited by the early imams, including Ali himself. Ali was succeeded by eleven direct male descendents. The Twelfth Imam, Muhammad, went into hiding at the age of four in 873 to begin a "long absence"—a kind of indefinite "spiritual hibernation." He is therefore the "Hidden Imam." A Shiite article of faith is that the last (twelfth) imam is waiting for an auspicious moment to reappear. His return will signal the re-establishment of a just and pure Islamic state—a replication of the Prophet's ideal umma.

During his absence, Shiites are led by "ayatollahs" ("signs of Allah"), well-trained and trusted teachers who interpret the law and creeds for their communities.

Another name for the Twelfth Imam is "Mahdi," the guided one. He is a messianic figure who will come at the end of time to bring a period of harmony and righteousness, a form of the Kingdom of God. Both Sunni and Shiite Muslims believe that Jesus will also come before the Day of Judgment to defeat the forces of the ad-Dajjal (the anti-Christ). The Islamic and the Christian traditions combine to have a just culmination of history at the end of the age.

So, while the concept of Mahdi is known in Sunni Islam, for Sunnis it refers to a more anonymous figure. For Shiites this messianic person is the twelfth Imam.

As a result of patronage by the Safawi dynasty in sixteenth-century Iran, Twelvers are the dominant form of Islam in Iran and nearby Iraq. Qum and Karbala are holy cities in the respective countries. Incidentally, it was thought by many Iranians that the exiled Khomenei was that "Hidden Imam" returning to redeem Iran and bring victory to the entire Muslim world. Strictly speaking, however, "ayatollahs" are representatives of the Twelfth Imam.

Ismailis

The Ismailis are usually considered a Shiite sect, but have a philosophical bent toward Gnosticism. This means that "secret knowledge" is received by one joining this sect and the adherent will believe in the dualism of good and evil, light and darkness. At times in the past, Ismailis have been a secret society.

They are often called "Seveners" because Muhammad Ibn Ismail was the seventh and last imam. The number "7" denotes completeness, perfection, and the end of a cycle. Its historic claim to fame was the Fatimi dynasty in Egypt from 969-1174 and the construction of the famous Al-Azhar University in Cairo. However, for centuries now, Al-Azhar has been free of all Ismaili influences.

As with all branches of Islam, Ismailis had a tendency to proliferate and there are many subgroups. An important branch of the Ismailis settled in Cairo in 909 and called themselves Fatimids. The Fatimid Caliphate claimed to be descendants of Muhammad and adopted the name of his daughter. The Fatimid Ismailis produced a small group called Druze, now primarily located in Syria. The Druze have made news in the past twenty years because of their role in Lebanon's civil war. The very wealthy family of the Aga Khan also constitutes a small Ismaili faction.

A brief mention should be made of the Assassins, one of the most notorious of Ismaili sects. The name is derived from the Arabic "user of hashish" (hashshashin). They were a twelfth- and thirteenth-century, primarily Syrian, phenomenon, which made them contemporaries of the Crusaders.

History has recorded them as fearless and fearful Muslims who employed terrorist tactics to further their vision of Islam. They were known as blindly obedient to their leaders.

What history does not record is their intellectual interests, their founding of libraries and their commitment to scientific study. They reflected the dualism, hidden knowledge, and secret truths of the Gnostic legacy in Ismaili thought. Their influence waned after large Mongol armies conquered Syria in 1256.

The Ismailis, as a group, are a much smaller branch of Shiites than the Twelvers and are found today mostly in India and Pakistan.

It is not appropriate to refer to Shiites as "fundamentalists." That is a loaded western word and media short-hand to describe a complex Muslim community. Contemporary Shiites must be understood as a religious movement seeking to return to an uncritical affirmation of the divinity of the Quran. This is normative Islam. By virtue of and in the name of that return, it is opposed to the multi-faceted secular materialistic forces it experiences from western culture. Eric Davis suggests the phrase: "Islamic radicalism" as an alternative to "Islamic fundamentalism."[18] It is a fairer description because, as we have seen, they want to reclaim the roots of Islam.

The underlying difference between Sunnis and Shiites is the source of leadership for the umma. Another more minor contrast is the Shiite emphasis on Ijtihad or reliance on reason as authoritative in legal matters. Khomenei was a product of this tradition and wrote several brilliant treatises on theological and philosophical subjects. Shiite "rationalism" is similar to the logical methodology of many conservative Catholic and Protestant theologians.

O God, break with thy blows this shell of self, until thy light is reflected in glory from the hidden mirror at the foundation of my soul.

A Sufi Prayer

These things we tell of can never be found by seeking, yet only seekers find it.

Bayazid al-Bistami, a Persian Sufi

The Sufi Dimension:
From the Aridity of Orthodoxy
to the Oasis of the Heart

My servant does not cease to approach me with acts
of devotion until I become the foot with which he
walks, the hand with which he grasps, and the eye
with which he sees. (Hadith)

No religion is complete without an ecstatic dimension.
Something in human beings wants to keep religion from being simply ritual, purely rational, solely ethical, and only
theology. So a corrective eventually expresses itself in the
form of mysticism (*Tasawwuf*). Mysticism is not the religion; it is an inescapable element in all authentic religions.
As Paul Tillich used to say, ecstasy and mysticism prevent
religion from becoming "moralized love and intellectualized
faith."

Most religious founders combine these dimensions in their
lives and thought. They emphasize that our relationship to
the Divine includes thinking and acting correctly and experiencing God directly. This is certainly true of Muhammad.
Sufis base their devotional expression and spiritual direction
on the example of the Prophet. Muhammad was the original
Sufi! They immediately point to his prayer life, his direct en-
counter with Allah on Mt. Hira, his spiritual pilgrimage in
his late thirties which led to his "Night of Power," and finally to his "Night Journey," a classical mystical experience
which took him to heaven to talk with previous prophets and

into the presence of Allah Himself. The Hadith is replete
with spiritual wisdom, and meditational guides which were
as much a part of Muhammad's legacy to his followers as
his political and ethical guidance.

Annemarie Schimmel, in her comprehensive book on
Sufism, *Mystical Dimensions of Islam,* relates how sur-
prised westerners are to discover the mystical qualities in
Muhammad. She states that the western image of Islam
"emerged during hundreds of years of hatred and enmity in
the Christian world." From this tradition has come a picture
of Muhammad, at worst, as a sword-wielding religious
zealot and, at best, a shrewd and sensuous politician.[19] Yet
from the beginning Sufis knew him to be a deeply pious and
spiritually earnest man, a man who not only desired to bring
Allah's Salam to earth, but who also experienced direct access to Allah.

Sufis are the "inner dimension" of Islam, the personal, esoteric, inward path (Tariqa) as compared with the esoteric,
public, outward Shariah. The former, "God and the person,"
is the inner essence; the latter, "God and society," is the ex-
terior clothing. The former is "fire"; the latter is the
"fireplace." Obviously both are needed for a viable religious
tradition. One without the other would be spiritually self-
destructive.

Sufism is not, as often stated by westerners, a sect of Islam.
It is, rather, a dimension found in and compatible with all
manifestations of Islam, whether it be Sunni or Shiite and

whatever the Muslims are, intelligentsia or peasant, urban or rural.

Sufi Islam shares some general traits with mysticism the world over. First, Sufi mystics are ascetic; they engage in self-renunciation, stressing simple-living and poverty. Unlike mystical traditions in other religions, such as Hinduism and Christianity, Sufis do not turn their back on the world. When the Sufi is united with God, his heart is admittedly changed; this, however, is not a private, other-worldly experience. The purpose of the transformation is so the Sufi can see the world as God sees it. Rather than escaping the world, he wants to be with God in the world.

Sufis may live in communities with their spiritual teacher and leader, the Sheik (Shaykh), but there are no monasteries. Islam is too concerned about the world and the ethical life to construct cloistered monastic cells. A visible symbol of their self-mortification is the coarse woolen cloth called *Suf*, which helped keep them warm during solitary vigils in the desert and from which they get their name.

Secondly, Sufis, like many theistic mystics, stress the Heart as the seat of comprehension, a way of knowing, and as a mode of seeking God. Sufi mysticism is often called the "path of love" and observers claim that Sufis have a "love affair" with God. Consistently, then, much Sufi literature is love poetry or "poetry of passion." It represents the longing of the Sufis to be with God, to find fulfillment in union with God, to be one with the Divine Beloved, who is the object of desire. A fine example of this form of mystical verse is from a prominent nineteenth-century Sufi poet, Fazil.

> So Love is the guide to the World Above, the stair leading up to the portal of Heaven; through the fire of Love, iron is transmuted into gold, and the dark day into a shining gem. Love it is that makes the heedless wise and changes the ignorant into an adept of the Divine mysteries; Love is the unveiler of the Truth, the hidden way into the Sanctuary of God. And as for the true Lover, he is pure of heart and holy of life, worldly things are of no account with him, dust and gold being equal in his eyes; generosity and gentleness distinguish him; carnal desire stirs him not.

Although obedience is stressed more in the Quran than love, Sufis, in devotion to their path and in their search for union with God, have unashamedly adopted love as the means to achieve the end they seek. Love ultimately leads to love.

The spiritual discipline of Remembrance (Dhikr) is another way Sufis arrive at their final goal of union with Allah.* The re-membering of God is a healing of our dis-membering as a result of our attachment to this world and our own ego. Since we have a tendency to forget, that greatest of sins, the Quran commands us to "remember."

---

*The "dh" in *Dhikr* is pronounced like the English "th," but many Arabs pronounce "dh" as "z."

Abu l-Qasim al-Qushayri outlines three stages in the practice of Remembrance. These stages are in order of progression and intensity of mystical vision:

1. Remembrance of the Tongue. Certain phrases are repeated in mantra fashion such as Allahu Akbar (God is Greatest) or one of the many other names of God or certain brief verses from the Quran. This process helps our mind to begin concentrating on God, rather than on the mundane and trivial.

2. Remembrance of the Heart. This more profound, inward meditation is a movement away from what we do, such as repeating words, to a focus on divine thoughts we find in the verses of the Quran. This second stage will, one hopes, erase further awareness of external stimuli and prepares us for the final stage.

3. Remembrance of the Secret. Now the disciple is at the center of his being, the place of immediate vision of God. Here there is effortless thought of God; the Sufi is in God and God is in him. Ecstatic union has been reached.

The greatest mystic-poet in Sufi history, Jalal ad-Din al Rumi (d. 1273), had an unforgettable image for this union. The mystic "who has lost himself in God has the signet that bears God's image."[20] Rumi also stresses the language and method of love. If the soul is lost in love, the ego is annihilated. He experienced this in love relationships and deep friendships. "There is no room for two I's in one house," he said in one of his famous tales.* Egolessness is a prerequisite for admission to the house of the lover as well as to the house of God.

Sufis called this experience *fana,* annihilation of the self, or the extinguishing of the ego. *Fana* really means the destruction of the self or ego from within, a gradual dissipation of the self so that the self is forgotten and God remembered. Many Muslim scholars suggest that annihilation is not a good translation of *fana* because it connotes destruction from above or from outside.

However the ego-less union with Allah was achieved, orthodox Muslims were offended by this blurring of lines between the creature and the Creator. They were sure the "otherness" of Allah had been compromised. They could not bear having someone so identified with God that distinction was no longer possible.

A few Sufis went so far as to claim they were God. Tenth-century Al-Hallaj was thought blasphemous for saying, "I am the Ultimate Reality," and was subsequently executed. Abu-Yazid, a ninth-century Sufi, after reaching mystical union with God said, "Praise be to me." The ordinary modes of perception based on subject-object duality no longer obtained. Consciousness was so purified that God "is all in all."

---

*There are many versions of this story, but the one recorded by Annemarie Schimmel on p. 314 in *Mystical Dimensions of Islam* is one of the most complete.

For some sects of Sufis, the practice of Dhikr is accompanied by dancing, called *Mawlawiyah*, after an order of Sufis founded by Al-Rumi. These Sufi dancers are also known as Whirling Dervishes. As the planets revolve around the sun, the brothers dance around a pillar, or more frequently around a Sheik, who acts as a "center of the world." The whirling dance and chanting Dhikr have the effect of helping the Sufi achieve alteration of consciousness and mystical ecstasy in a more rapid and certain manner. Music also is played for the dancing, a rarity for Muslim worship.

Most western acquaintance with Sufi mysticism is through viewing the dervishes' dancing exhibitions as they tour annually the major cities in America. This is, of course, a public replication of their devotion, but does give us a sense of the Sufi dimension of Islam.

In summary, faithful Muslims who are not Sufis obey God and believe that God is merciful and will reward them according to their righteous deeds. The goal is to enjoy life in this world and prepare for the world to come. They diligently perform the five pillars, and this aids them in "remembering Allah." However, their self-renunciation and abstinence do not go beyond their expected duties and obligations.

Sufis, on the other hand, passionately yearn for God. Their remembrance is total, a struggle (Jihad) to be united with Divine Love. The Sufi's goal is not to perform certain rituals and hope thereby to become closer to God; his goal is to be united to God without any mediation whatsoever. A Sufi does not neglect action; he sees it as a completion of action. There is a sense in which Sufis see themselves as "fulfilled Muslims."

The Balanced Sufi: Abu Hamid Muhammad al-Ghazali

Al-Ghazali (d. 1111) is considered one of the greatest scholars in the history of Islam. He approximated the ideals of the Prophet in the same way St. Francis imitated Jesus.

He was born in Tus, Persia, and after passing his theological courses with distinction, this brilliant student became a professor at age thirty-three in the university at Baghdad.

After five years of successful teaching, he began to experience episodes of spiritual distress he called a "disease" and an "unhealthy condition." He knew about God, but he did not know God. Thoroughly dissatisfied, he abandoned teaching and engaged in a vigorous self-examination. He concluded, "'the teacher must be taught," or as Montgomery Watt said, "the teacher of religion needs to become a religious man."

His self-criticism carried him to criticism of all the ways one knows Truth and God. He dismissed sense perception as deceiving, theology as limited rational discourse about God, philosophy as vain speculation apart from Revelation, and authoritative answers as too non-critical. All these roads were dead ends; his last step on the journey of honest doubt and spiritual anxiety was another path altogether—the Sufi way.*

What impressed him about the mystics was their capacity to circumvent theology and sense perception and experience God directly. The Sufis helped him see with another eye, the eye of intuition, or to use al-Ghazali's word, to "taste" God. This sense of immediacy with God was what he had sought.

But there was an instinctive sense of balance in al-Ghazali. The joy and certainty that accompanied his immediacy with God did not force him to abandon theology. He came back to the center of Islam and integrated the rational and intuitive, the intellectual and the practical, the mystical and the theological.

He captured this centering in a book called *The Just Balance*. Al-Ghazali would never make the outrageous claim: "I am God," as some Sufis did. His Islamic balance made him virtually unassailable by mainstream Muslims—but Islam has never been the same since al-Ghazali. He combined theology and mysticism with such power and integrity that it was imperative ever since for every orthodox theologian and Muslim scholar to take Sufism seriously.

---

*Al-Ghazali's appreciation of the Sufi path is seen in the following observation: "It became clear to me, however, that what is most distinctive of mysticism is something which cannot be apprehended by study, but only by immediate experience *(dhawq*—literally, 'tasting'), by ecstasy and by a moral change." Montgomery Watt, *The Faith and Practices of Al-Ghazali*. Chicago: Kazi Publications, 1982, p. 55.

Part Three

Some Current Issues

The Status of Women

Paradise lies at the feet of mothers. (Hadith)

All human beings (male and female) are equal, equal as the teeth of a comb. There is no superiority of a white over a black nor of any male over the female. Only the God-consciousness (regardless of gender) merit favor and the ultimate rewards from God. (Muhammad)

With the possible exception of Jihad, the place of women in Islam is the most misunderstood notion by westerners. To be sure, Saudi Arabia, a few Gulf States, and increasingly Sudan and Pakistan combine their strong patriarchal tradition with the most conservative interpretation of Islamic law regarding women. As a result, from a western point of view, women often face unusual discrimination. But it should be said at the outset that the treatment of women in these countries is less a reflection of the Quran and more an expression of a cultural tradition which has inevitably been deferential to men.

Women's place in Muslim countries is as complex an issue as the status of women in Christian countries. A discussion of women and Islam must be seen in the context of class, country, and above all, the Quran. It is more accurate to say what a particular country does not permit women to do than to say what Islam permits or forbids.

The latter half of the twentieth century has seen a revival of extremely reactionary movements in Muslim countries, especially in and around the Middle East. Whenever that happens, women have often lost the status to which the Quran elevated them. Conversations with persons who have spent part of the last decade in Pakistan, Sudan, Egypt, and Arab Gulf States have confirmed this. Saudi Arabia and Iran represent this trend also.

But we hear little about the diversity of women's opportunities in Islamic countries and the flexibility of Islam as it moves from patriarchal cultures to democratic countries to the matriarchal societies of Indonesia and sub-Saharan Africa. We hear less about how women's traditional place is changing, what the Quran really says about women, and how many Muslim women are doctors, computer scientists, engineers, teachers, and bankers. The prominence of "class" in determining the destiny of Muslim women is also ignored. The poverty of most Muslim families compound whatever other religious and political status women might have.

The Quran and Women: Historical Context

Two-thirds of women in pre–Islamic society were slaves. They had no rights or legal and social status. Female infanticide was common. Men could have an unlimited number of wives and divorce them for no apparent reason with impunity. Inheritance always went to adult male relatives.

Islam and the Quran created major improvements in the status of women. They were oases in a desert of misogyny. The Quranic ideals, however, were not always translated into practice. The relative emancipation of women found in Islamic scripture has been seriously diluted by longstanding habits of male domination and cultural attitudes. Judaism and Christianity do not need reminding that cultural and secular interests can prevail over religious values.

Non–Muslim and Muslim societies forget the strong women of the early Islamic period—the successful business woman Khadija, the religious influence of Aisha and Fatima—and the fact that women participated in the army in early Islam. Allah was so concerned about the place of women that there is more said in the Quran about that than any other social issue. One of the longest Suras is entitled "Women" and in this case, the title represents the main content of the chapter.

The Quran and Women: Echo of Culture

There was in the Quran, just as in every divine text of major world religions, a reflection of cultural devaluation of women which appears restrictive and discriminatory to many Muslim and Western women.

1. Women's testimony is worth half of man's especially in civil cases. This is an attempt to forego distraction from family responsibilities and to protect women from the rigor and discomfort of prolonged trials. It also reflects a feeling that woman's emotional nature may prevent her from being as objective as men. On the other hand, in criminal cases, a woman's testimony carries as much weight as a man's.

2. Her share of inheritance is one-half of a male relative in the same category. This apparent inequity is justified because men have the obligation to provide for a family and will need extra income. Since women may keep whatever dowry they receive, there is a hope that income level will ultimately be fair. (See 4:7-12, 176)

3. There is no polyandry (more than one husband), but polygyny (more than one wife) has continued.

4. The husband is the head of the household, is the final authority, and has due obedience and cooperation from his wife. If the wife is rebellious or disobedient, there are several options open to the husband. He may first try to dissuade her with kind and gentle reasoning. If this fails, he

may then refrain from sleeping with her. And if the above are not effective, he has the Quranic permission to "beat her slightly." (4:34)

Such "slight physical correction" (Yusuf Ali) avoids her face and other sensitive areas. Striking your wife in the face (as was pictured in the film *Not Without My Daughter*) and other forms of verbal and physical cruelty have no sanction in the Quran. Many Muslims feel that although permitted, this activity is not advisable and is the exception much more than the rule.

If all else fails, the next verse (35) suggests the couple seek help and counsel from a mediator. Perhaps the disagreement between husband and wife can be resolved in this open, balanced, and neutral way.[21]

Seclusion and the Veil

In the traditional societies of the Middle East, women are not socially independent. They need men to act on their behalf. They ask men's permission to leave home; and they are often secluded from male visitors to the home. Women cannot be imams, although they can lead prayer services for women in their homes. On the other hand, Sufi societies allow women to be religious leaders and are generally more positive about all aspects of womanhood.

The aforementioned reference to seclusion needs some elaboration. It is often called "veiling" or *purdah,* another word for seclusion. The rigidity with which it is held depends on the country involved. It is most prevalent in Saudi Arabia, Afghanistan, and post-revolutionary Iran, but to some degree it is present in most Muslim societies. Actually, purdah and complete veiling are Persian and Indian customs which, in time, many neighboring countries adopted. There is one verse in the Quran which mentions veiling: "Prophet, enjoin your wives, your daughters, and the wives of true believers to draw their veils close round them. That is more proper so they may be recognized and not molested." (35:59 also 24:30-31) The historical context for what is "proper" is that Arabian women before Islam were scantily attired and often topless; as a result, they were abused by men.

The primary concern of the Quran is modesty in dress. "Drawing the veil close round them" had the intention of preventing promiscuity and arousing men's desire, but most of all it guarded against disrespect of women and violence against them.

Although "veiling" is barely mentioned in the Quran, it is a form of status among contemporary wealthy educated Egyptian women to wear a *ghata*, a kind of scarf which exposes only the face. For others in Iran and Saudi Arabia, where most of the body is covered, it is a matter of religious obedience.

Jane Smith, formerly of Harvard Center for the Study of World Religions and now Dean of Academic Affairs at Iliff School of Theology of Denver, has a helpful perspective on why Muslim women dress the way they do:

Regardless of their degree of liberation, Muslim women value modesty as well as prize and retain their femininity. They find particularly odious, as do Muslim men, the sexual permissiveness of Western society. Whether the control exercised by Muslim men over their women is viewed as protection or exploitation, the fact remains that liberal and conservative Muslims alike are appalled and disgusted by women's open display of themselves and the sexual freedoms seen as part of the general emancipation of women in the West.... To cite the expressive commentary of Fatima Mernissi, "While Muslim exploitation of the female is clad under veils and buried behind walls, Western exploitation has the bad taste of being unclad, bare and overexposed."*[22]

*It would be only fair to record that Muslims see Christianity as counseling women also to be obedient, modest in dress, submissive to husbands, and quiet in church. This restrictive teaching is akin to Quranic legislation. See Colossians 3:18, Ephesians 5:24, I Peter 2:1-6, I Timothy 2:5-12, and I Corinthians 14:34-35.

The Quran and Women: Challenge to Culture

However inadequate these above-mentioned teachings and practices seem to be, they were a significant step forward. Comparatively speaking, against the backdrop of seventh-century Arabia, the Quran was a virtual champion of women's rights. Much of what the Quran advocates for women was not seen in the West until approximately a hundred years ago. Many Muslim women of this century are reclaiming rights and a status given them by the Quran, but whittled away during the last fourteen hundred years. Here is a list of teachings from the Quran to which many Muslims point with pride.

1. Female infanticide was abolished.

2. Primogeniture, when inheritance goes only to the oldest male heir, was banned.

3. Men must pay a dowry to their wives. This money went to the wife, not her father, and it was her private property to do with as she saw fit. Moreover, she was able to keep it even after a divorce.

4. Women could inherit property from husbands and fathers.

5. Women could retain their maiden names.

6. Divorce may be initiated by women according to the Quran after sincere attempts to preserve marriage are made and as a last resort.

7. Husbands must sign marriage contracts to indicate how much they are willing to pay their wives in event of divorce.

8. Pre-nuptial agreements may include conditions set by a wife and they must be honored.

9. Women have final approval on a marriage partner arranged by her parents.

10. Widows have the right to remarry and are encouraged to do so.

11. Religious equality of sexes before God and intellectual equality before humankind are affirmed. Both have equal access to heaven: "Whosoever does good deeds, whether male or female, while being believers, they shall enter paradise." (4:124, 40:40)

There are two verses in the Quran which state the inherent equality of men and women in Allah's act of creation: "O Mankind, reverence your Guardian and Lord Who created you from a single Person, created of like nature and from them twain scattered countless men and women" (4:1), and a similar passage in 39:6: "He created you from a single Person; Then created, of like nature, his mate."

The logic of this equality in creation means that "women shall have rights similar to the rights against them according to what is equitable." (2:228) The Quran goes on to say in the same verse that men have a "degree of advantage" over women. This seeming imbalance refers not to superiority, but to functional difference. The husband's obligation to provide economic well-being for his family gives him the right to be in charge (4:34). This was never meant to be exploitative or to result in political advantage for the man. In any case, the Islamic doctrine of *tawhid* is at work here— equality before God implies equality before each other.

12. Muslim men were and are limited to four wives. Polygamy is never encouraged in the Quran. In fact, monogamy is the preferred state and Quranic ideal. The husband is permitted additional wives only on the condition that he is able to treat each wife equally, fairly, and justly, and only if the family, as a unit, will not suffer by the addition of wives (4:3). To prevent exploitation of women and the selfishness of men, the latter may be required to apply for permission before a matrimonial counsel to marry again. So, from the point of view of the Quran, taking a second wife is a solemn agreement to accept certain serious responsibilities. Since it is very difficult to treat each wife impartially, less than 2% of Muslim marriages are polygamous. This means monogamy is the rule.

In early Islam, there was a historic basis and social need for polygamy—to protect the security of surplus women.* A metaphysical basis was soon offered by Muslim scholars to explain polygamy. The Oneness of the Male Principle was joined by a multiplicity of Divine Infinitude in the form of Females. This helped to preserve polygamy as an institution, but the Quranic ideal of monogamy was the final arbiter of how women should fare in marriage.

Islam did provide legal rights for women, especially in the area of family life. Quranic advocacy of women and its correction of the harsh treatment women typically received in the seventh century, contains a strong sense of prophetic justice.

From a western standpoint, the Quran may not outline an even playing field for men and women. When seen from within the society of Islam, however, men and women are less opposites and more complements to the other. The sensitivity of Jane Smith provides fresh insight to a problem endemic to world religions. It is worth quoting in its entirety:

> It is my opinion that Western feminists are beginning
> to recognize what historians of religion were a long
> time in realizing—that the kinds of assumptions one

---

*The Roman Catholic Church is facing the same problem today in parts of Africa. Social and economic reasons are forcing the Church to reconsider polygamy as a Christian option. See *Polygamy Reconsidered* by Eugene Hillman, New York: Orbis Press, 1973.

brings to the observation of another culture often lead to the asking of questions basically inappropriate to that culture. We must begin to listen more carefully to what persons from within cultural traditions, in this case particularly women, are saying in response to their own felt needs and priorities. The point has been made repeatedly that the history of women in Islam reveals a clear pattern of male domination. But what I have tried to indicate is that from within the Islamic perspective this is a divinely-initiated and therefore natural and right circumstance. In all religions the rules have been made by men, insist Western feminists, and women must play the parts thus determined for them. But for the Muslim women this is not necessarily the case. Listen again to my Egyptian friend:

> [Western feminists] say that the rules have been made by men for women to follow. But they do not understand that Muslim women believe these to be divine rules.... By liberating them from these 'man-made' regulations they are in fact liberating them from their own religion.[23]

Human Rights

The easiest way to understand Islam and human rights is to heed an observation by the Egyptian scholar Sayyid Qutb. He reminds us that from its beginning, Islam had a strong egalitarian streak; it owed allegiance to no king or government. It had the unique opportunity of starting without major competition or resistance, thus having the luxury of being itself. As a result of this unusual freedom, "Islam chose to unite earth and heaven in one spiritual organization, and one that recognized no difference between worldly zeal and religious coercion."[24]

Islam never intends to fracture the unity Qutb calls a "two-in-one-society." Social justice (politics) and personal freedom (religion) are never divorced. Both are under obedience to Allah. We in the West tend to separate these dimensions of life in the name of the Enlightenment and democracy. When we see a society governed by religious law such as Shariah and the Quran, we call it a theocracy, that is, a God-ruled society. But this has little meaning to a Muslim. Of course, God should rule a country through His proper servants. The common people do not have the authority and wisdom to make decisions for everyone or to make public policy. They could easily be wrong. Sovereignty in Islam inherently belongs not to the people, but to God.

In a society where God's word is Law, it is more accurate to talk of duties, not rights. Caliphs, fathers, and imams have duties to see that all people for whom they are responsible attain the fullest humanity Allah expects. Then they would have what the West calls "rights"—life, religion, ownership of property, and human dignity.

Human individual rights do not exist apart from God. There is no independent source which grants "rights"; a separate source would constitute idolatry. If Islam is the final dispenser of Allah's Law, which affects all of life, it follows that what the Quran says about human rights must be obeyed.

As we review Islam's position on human rights, we must keep in mind the variety of Islam's expressions throughout the world—from Morocco to Indonesia. As with Islam's views on women, our opinions are too often formed based on media images, often anecdotal and isolated, and from the Middle East.

Let's examine some Quranic verses for a basis of Muslim tolerance for differences in people. One can appreciate, for instance, the disdain of the Quran for verbal ridicule and name-calling. Words can seem innocent enough, but they also can be breeding grounds for acts of violence. Sura 49:11 says, "O ye who believe, let not some men among you laugh at others: It may be that the latter are better than the former... Nor defame nor be sarcastic to each other. Nor call each other by offensive nicknames." This call for the expansion of human sensitivity and plea for attitudinal change can often nip inappropriate behavior in the bud.

Another verse in the same vein goes, "Behold God enjoins justice and the doing of good, and generosity towards one's fellow men, and He forbids all that is shameful and all that runs counter to reason, as well as envy; He exhorts you so that you bear this in mind." (16:90) It is considered unreasonable to devalue another person in any way. Fazlur Rahman said that Allah's gift of human reason appears in its "most perverted form when it attempts to establish the superiority of one group over another."

From this sampling of texts and from the Prophet's example, one can see how racism is virtually unknown in Islam. Indifference to color and race was congenital with the new religion. The only wife other than Khadija by whom Muhammad had a child was a Copt from Egypt. Bilal, a black slave, was one of his first and most committed converts and the first person to chant the call to prayer in 622. By precept and example, Muslims are forbidden to be prejudiced against someone because of their race. It is not accidental that of all the Biblical religions, Islam is the most successful among people of color.

The classical text used to guarantee freedom of religion and ideological expression is 2:256: "Let there be no compulsion in religion." Every commentator on this verse insists that profession of religion must be a voluntary decision, and that forced religion is a contradiction in terms. Yusuf Ali says that compulsion is incompatible with religion.

How does Islam negotiate "freedom of religion" on the one hand and its claim to be the final Truth of Allah on the other? A three-tiered approach was devised to achieve peaceful cooperation with various populations in an Islamic State. First of all, there is the Muslim majority composed of believers who enjoy full rights under Shariah Law. Then there are the Jews and Christians (called dhimmis)—People of the Book or Fellow Covenanters—mentioned in an earlier chapter. Because of this special relation to Islam, they are afforded special protection. All that is required of them is payment of taxes to the state for the services they receive. A third category is the "associates"; sometimes in history they were called "enemies." These were usually non-monotheists who rejected both conversion to Islam or affinity with People of the Book. The "associates" have been variously treated throughout history depending of the flexibility of the administration of Shariah Law. In reality, the ideals of justice, equality and freedom found in Islam are sometimes relatively applied to minorities in a Muslim community. Again it depends where you are and on what form of Islamic government is in power. As with all religions, the practice does not always measure up to its profession. Human beings often arrogate to themselves a sense of divine authority and speak for themselves rather than God.

Furthermore, just as we cannot stretch First Amendment freedoms irresponsibly, freedom has its limits in Islamic society. Freedom of speech and assembly are guaranteed as long as they do not subvert Islam or violate the Quran or Shariah Law. Evil and blasphemy are not permitted. From an Islamic point of view, Salman Rushdie committed religious treason by writing heretical material as an apostate Muslim. Freedom and human rights take place within the framework of a state attempting to live the Law of Islam.

I should hasten to add that Muslim emphasis on religious freedom is not meant to be patronizing or to be a concession to non-believers. It is a fundamental right granted by God. The ideal Muslim society existed, it is believed, in the early years of Islam. Muslims look to that standard and not to how fallibly it has been embodied to measure their faithfulness. What we understand to be human rights, fundamental equality and justice, freedom of conscience and expression, are operating principles in the Quran and practical concerns for the Muslim (5:9).

Part Four

Islam's Gifts to the West

Islam's major legacy to the world is the gift of its religion. That would have been quite sufficient in itself. But there are many other assets spawned by this religious tradition which deserve recognition and which daily influence our lives.

This chapter focuses on the debt westerners owe Islam for contributions from the Middle East during the Golden Age of Islam. The extent of this debt goes far beyond the brevity of this chapter.

Techniques of irrigation developed by Muslims working in the Fertile Crescent were imitated by European farmers. Muslims were excellent cartographers; their maps were far more accurate than those of Europe. Arabs brought paper into Europe. They invented the pointed arch without which the Gothic cathedral would have been impossible. Note the vaulted ceilings, the endlessly unfolding arcades, and high-niched portals found in many Muslim buildings, especially mosques and palaces. Furthermore, under the inspiration of Islam, Arabs were known for various forms of ornamentation, carving, weaving, damask, embossing, leather craft, wood and metal work.

I want to highlight several major contributions of this Golden Age—from the eighth to the thirteenth centuries—when Muslim culture was far superior to that of Christian Europe.

Art

Although there was a rich tradition of poetry in pre–Islamic Arabia, the latter's artistic heritage was as culturally barren as much of the desert which surrounded it. While much of Islamic art was a result of creative borrowing from cultures it conquered or from peoples with whom it traded, the aesthetic dimension of Islam itself was not stifled. It was as much a response to God as any other dimension of life.

Although the prohibition against "graven images" was not from the Quran, a strong tradition forbidding the depiction of human figures was based on the Prophet's words in the Hadith. He once found Aisha decorating a pillow with a human figure and replied, "Don't you know that angels refuse to enter a house in which there is a picture? On the Last Day makers of pictures will be punished, for God will say to them, 'Give life to that which you have created.' " In representing human beings as "living creatures," artists are competing with God who alone makes living things. It is this fear of idolatry that explains why orthodox Jews are suspicious of being photographed and why so much of Islamic art gives expression to impersonal, abstract designs.

There are many exceptions to the rule. One, of course, is the "Night Journey" of Muhammad to heaven which is frequently a subject of illustration. Another exception is the numerous very colorful Persian miniatures which depict renditions of humans and animals. Persian and Turkish artists, who did not inherit the Semitic antipathy toward representational art, often produced whole books illustrating the life of the Prophet. Nevertheless, it should be made clear that no human image is found in a mosque.

The traditional prohibition against painting and sculpting human beings did not suppress the Muslims' artistic imagination. It simply went in the direction of the impersonal and abstract. If the real world was beyond their pale, then the unreal world would be made visible. In place of direct representation, there emerged wonderfully abstract designs which broke ties with the concrete world and led viewers to a world beyond themselves. Unlike Michelangelo's *David,* which tends to focus one's attention on David or the sculptor, the indirect, stylized, impersonal abstract art of Islam symbolizes a transcendent reality, or as Muslims would say "points to the glory of God." These patterns of art were found everywhere—on ceramic tiles, lacquered boxes, carpets, vases, and friezes.

The abstract designs took three basic forms.

1. Geometrical. This style of ornamentation was constructed with straight lines revealing the Muslim fascination with mathematics. Illuminations of the Quran and decorations of mosques were made showing mathematical certainty and regularity. The intricacy of these geometric shapes expressed the imaginative use of overlaying squares, rectangles, trian-gles, hexagons, and octagons. Throughout the designs are seen balance, symmetry, and order.

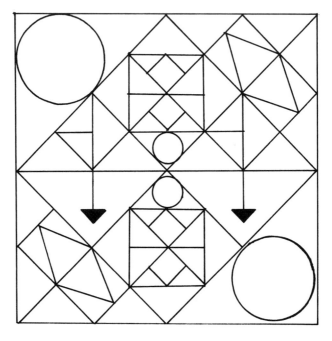

Example of geometric symmetry in Islamic abstract art, created by Jody Kathryn Zepp.

2. Vegetal. This form of abstraction was often called *Arabesque*. Al-Faruqi suggests four basic elements to Arabesque: 1) its fear of *shirk* (idolatry), 2) its repetitive-ness, 3) its symmetry, and 4) its momentum. Concerning the latter point, there is a sense of motion in Arabesque figures that never seems to end (such as in our twirling barbershop poles). It appears to continue beyond natural limits to infinity, and that, in fact, is one of the main objectives of the intricate freedom of Arabesque.

The interconnecting lines, interlacing rosettes, intertwining vines, interweaving curves—all portray growth, change, and movement. The fluidity of these designs reflects the unity of creation and the unity of Allah as well as the dynamism of history which is central to Abrahamic religion.

Example of vegetal arabesque abstract art, by Jody Kathryn Zepp.

3. Calligraphic. Since the religion of Islam was so dependent on the written word, writing became a sacred art to Islam (96:4). The religion of the Book inspired countless calligraphers to make the Word of God visible and optically pleasing. Calligraphy is Arabesque for the reader. It was the most noble, important, and appreciated art form in Islam, precisely because of its association with the Quran. Some say it is the "heartbeat of Muslim art." Calligraphy and Recitation of the Quran are vocations held in the highest esteem in Islam.

The calligraphers' favorite portions of the Quran are the *Bismillah* (In the Name of Allah, the Most Merciful, the

Most Compassionate), the *Shahadah* (There is no God but God and Muhammad is the Prophet of God), and the *Fatiha* (the first Sura). To calligraph these verses is to embellish the Heavenly Book, Divinity itself. Some obvious parallels in the West are illuminated manuscripts such as the ornamentation on the pages of the *Book of Kells* and *Lindisfarne Gospels* and the icons of the Eastern Orthodox Church.

Calligraphy of Quranic verses is a way of praising God without picturing God. It is really a form of communicating the Word of God as much as it is an art form. That is why so much of it appears on walls, facades, and domes of mosques. Julie Badiee, who teaches Islamic art at Western Maryland College, says "Calligraphy of the Quran can be thought analagous to the images of Christ in a Christian church."

The elegant script, exaggerated flourishes, and finely turned letters help us experience transcendence and see the "otherness" of words we are reading. Richard Martin rightly concludes that "calligraphy is the ultimate achievement in the Islamic arts."[25] Architecture is the penultimate art form.

Architecture

The Muslim engineer's creative genius is expressed in the
Red Fort in Delhi, the Alhambra in Grenada, and the Taj
Mahal in Agra. But it is the mosque which remains the Muslim architect's lasting monument. As a tribute to Islamic ar-
chitects, mosques have been called "calligraphy in architectural form." Others have called these sanctuaries and places
of prayer "theology in concrete."

Mosques are undoubtedly some of the world's most fascinating and attractive buildings. There is a sober and unosten-
tatious beauty about them, an unassuming sublimity, and a
singular lack of tension which reinforces the believer's in-
stinct to be reverent in the presence of the Holy.

The Prophet wanted the mosque to be a plain and simple
building very much like his home in Medina which served as
the first mosque and remained the model for all succeeding
mosques: an open courtyard and enclosed place for prayer in
front of the qibla. But as the new religion expanded and architectural influences made their way into Islam, mosques
became more decorative and elaborate. In whatever cultural
tradition mosques found themselves, they retained their distinctive beauty, be it the Arab-style mosque of Cordoba, the

Turkish Blue Mosque in Istanbul, or the Persian Masjid-i Shah mosque in Isfahan.

Taj Mahal in Agra, India. Built by Shah Jahan in tribute to his wife, Mumtaz Mahal. Completed in 1648. [Photo by Julie Badiee]

As Holly Edwards says in *Patterns and Precision: The Arts and Sciences of Islam,* "More than any other art form, architecture proclaims the faith. Silhouetted against the skyline, the dome and the minaret announce the vital presence of Islam."[26]

Silhouetted minarets of the Sultan Ahmad Mosque (The Blue Mosque), Istanbul, built in 1617. [Photo by Heshmat Badiee]

While the structure of a mosque may vary from culture to culture, there are basic elements which remain constant. "Mosque" (the Arabic is *masjid*) literally means "place of prostration" or "a place of prayer." All other features of the building accommodate this primary function.

There is a flat open space in which men (sometimes women) stand in line to perform *salat*, the daily prayer. On the wall which the worshipers face is a concave space, an arched niche (*Mihrab*) which indicates the direction of Mecca. This orientation point (*Qibla*) for prayer is essential for every mosque. Near the mihrab is the pulpit (*Minbar*) with a staircase on which the imam stands for the sermon at Friday noon prayers.

In the middle of the courtyard or garden in front of the mosque is a fountain or trough which is used for ritual ablutions, a requirement before prayers. Near the mosque or often attached to it are towers called *minarets*. The muezzin climbs one of them to call the faithful to prayer. Removing your shoes before entering a mosque reflects God's word to Moses as he approached the Burning Bush: "Take off your shoes; for the ground on which you stand is holy ground." To create a place of quiet reverential dignity is the aim of every Muslim architect as he designs a mosque.

Masjid-i-Shah in Isfahan, Iran. *Masjid* is Arabic
for mosque. [Photo by Lucille Oeming]

The Alhambra in Granada, Spain. Of fourteenth-century construction, it is claimed to be the zenith of Islamic architecture in the West. [Photo courtesy of Aramco World]

Badshahi Mosque in Lahore, Pakistan. Built in 1674, it contains one of the most symmetrical facades of any mosque. [Photo courtesy of Information Division, Embassy of Pakistan, Washington, D.C.]

Dome of the Rock in Jerusalem. The oldest surviving Islamic monument, built by ibn Mauwan in 690. Today it is more a sanctuary than a mosque. [Photo courtesy of Aramco World]

Sciences*

As we have seen, while the Western world was living through the Middle Ages, Islam was experiencing a "Golden Age" or "Classical Period." No other time, including Periclean Athens and seventeenth-century Europe, produced more geniuses in Mathematics, Physics, and Medicine.

Baghdad was the intellectual center of this world. The universities founded at this time became models for much later European ones. All the available scholarship from Greece and the East was gathered in an institution called "The House of Wisdom." It was founded by the enlightened caliph Mamun who ruled in Baghdad from 813 to 833. Many of the Muslim scientists who taught or trained there were links between the ancient world and the European Renaissance. In fact, much of classical Greek knowledge was known to western scholars *only* through Arab translations. They literally "saved" these works for us. Raphael recognized this link when he included Muslims in his famous painting cel-

---

*I have depended heavily on Cyril Glassé's *A Concise Encyclopedia of Islam* and Ismail and Lois L. Faruqi's *A Cultural Atlas of Islam* for much of the following discussion. Another helpful resource was Muhammad Saud's *Islam and Evolution of Science* (Karachi, Shamsi Publishing Company, 1986).

ebrating the history of knowledge entitled "The School of
Athens."

The Al-Azhar in Cairo (founded in 970), the oldest Islamic
university in continual use. [Photo courtesy of Aramco World]

Physics

Muslims invented the clock pendulum, the magnetic compass, and the astrolabe. They also were first to create instruments to measure special weights and gravities of elements and did so with great precision. Much of this scientific methodology was the fruit of the Quran's condemnation of magic, superstition, and astrology, which gave humans freedom to explore and explain the universe rationally. The goal of Islamic scholarship from that time was to combine religious sciences and empirical sciences as another way of expressing tawhid.

Ibn al Haytham (d. 1039), sometimes called Alhazen in the West, was the first to suggest the damming of the Nile River at Aswan, a project accomplished in the twentieth century. He pioneered studies in atmospheric pressure and was the first to explain the rainbow scientifically.

He is considered the founder of optics, and by far his most famous achievements were in this field. Haytham's excellent studies on the reflection and refraction of light refuted the conventional wisdom from the Greeks that vision is caused by a ray sent from the eye which strikes the object and then returns to the eye.

Mathematics

Muslim scientists were at home with mathematics. Their sophistication in this discipline helped them to pioneer work in astronomy and other natural sciences. In their mathematical legacy is the letter "x" for an unknown quantity. Muslim scholars also developed and transmitted plane geometry and trigonometry to the West.

Muhammad ibn Musa al-Khwarizmi (d. 850). This Persian scientist invented algebra (*al-jabr*) which in Arabic means "to restore broken parts." All beginning algebra students experience this "bringing together" of reality in the form of equations. The Latin translation of his works introduced algebra to Europe.

After the zero was borrowed from India, Al-Khwarizmi established a system of counting which became known as Arabic numerals.

Medicine

By the tenth century a fully staffed medical school and hospital was located in Baghdad. Al-Faruqi records that it had outpatient clinics, pharmacies, and libraries. The first hospital was built in 706 and was the Johns Hopkins and Mayo Clinic of its time. In 931, eight hundred and sixty-nine physicians took their medical examinations and sought licenses to practice in Baghdad.

There are several medical firsts claimed for Islam by Muslim scholars:

1. the use of anesthesia in surgery

2. the cauterizing of wounds

3. the discovery that epidemics arise from contagion through touch and air

4. ambulatory hospitals carried on a camel's back (a kind of eighth-century MASH)

5. the separation of pharmacology from medicine and the writing of prescriptions

Because of this excellent preparation by a progressive medical school, tenth-century Muslim physicians were setting bones, performing surgery for cancer, removing cataracts, and operating on the human skull. Frequency of eye disease in the desert forced physicians to develop the science of ophthalmology.

Abu Bakr Muhammad al-Razi (d. 925) was the greatest physician in the Middle Ages. Like so many Islamic scientists of this Golden Age, he was, to use a later Western term, a Renaissance man, being well-versed in the fields of music, philosophy, and medicine. He wrote an encyclopedia of all medical facts known by his time. This monument to human knowledge was translated into Latin in 1486—the first medical book published in Europe.

His particular contributions to medicine were music therapy, the differentiation between smallpox and measles, the relation of sunstroke to circulation of blood, and the study of pediatrics.

Literature

Poetry was the Arabs' primary aesthetic interest, and seasonal fairs in Makkah (Mecca) and other centers provided occasion for competitions between the poets of the region. This vying for poetic-verbal supremacy generated in the citizenry an interest more passionate and more widespread than that aroused by the soccer or football matches of modern times in Western society.

Al-Faruqi, *The Cultural Atlas of Islam,* p. 357

As we mentioned earlier, the Arabic language has been indelibly influenced by the Quran. In turn, the style, syntax, and grammar of that language are measured by the standard set in the Quran. Its use of hyperbole and verbal eloquence build on and greatly enhance the Arabian propensity for graceful rhetoric. Quranic linguistic style influenced all sorts of literature—from letter writing among statesmen to poetry to stories like those in the *Arabian Nights.*

Poetry

The cultural interest of the masses was poetry, which resonated with the Arab soul the way singing does with the Welsh. It is not accidental, given the strong Arabic tradition of poetry, that the Quran was recited in poetic form.

SADI, HAFEZ, and RUMI

Al-Faruqi says that the "greatest poets of this time were the greatest poets of all time." These three Persian Sufi poets were probably the most highly regarded in both Islam and the West. Shamas al-Din Muhammad Hafez (d. 1391) and Muslah ad-Din Sadi (d. 1252) lived in Shiraz. Hafez wrote a significant collection of poems, called *Diwan* in Persian. Sadi wrote two famous poems: "The Fruit Garden" and "The Garden."

Arguably, the best and most important of these Persian Sufi poets was Jalal ad-Din al-Rumi. He was celebrated for his *ghazals*, poems in which human love is lyrically united with his Sufi spirituality. He also had his own *Diwan* or collection of poems.

But Rumi's masterpiece was *Mathnawi*, a 26,000-verse poem of epic proportions. A Mathnawi is a Persian poem composed of rhyming couplets which describes themes of love, teaching, and heroic endeavors.

Schimmel records a few couplets to give us a taste of Rumi's *Diwan*:

> Open the veil and close our door—
> You are and I, and empty the house.

> Without your speech the soul has no ear,
> Without your ear the soul has no tongue.

In another set of lines, Rumi uses the mercantile metaphors from the Quran to describe our relationship to God.

> With God is the best bargain; he buys from you your
> dirty fortune and gives in exchange light of the soul.
> He buys the ice of the perishable body and gives a
> kingdom beyond imagination.

Schimmel calls Rumi the "most inspired writer among the Muslim mystics."[27]

OMAR KHAYYAM

I want to briefly highlight Omar Khayyam (d. 1125) because of his popularity in the West. He lived in Naishapur in Persia and was known in his lifetime for being a mathematician and astronomer and a poet. In 1079, with a group of fellow scientists, he helped reform the Persian solar calendar. It was so accurate that it would lose only one day every 3770 years, but for some reason, it was never used.

Along the way Omar had written hundreds of four-lined poems (*rubaiyat*); after his death, many more were attributed to him. These quatrains were uneven in quality, but when British Victorian poet Edward Fitzgerald read them, he decided to put them into English verse.

The *Rubaiyat* contains a good deal of moralizing, sentimentality, and sensuous imagery as well as a curious mixture of philosophy, including pantheism, skepticism, predestination, and epicureanism. What is most appealing is probably Omar's apparent love of human and natural beauty. But as popular as it is among Western readers, Omar's poetry was virtually ignored by his peers.

Cyril Glassé notes that the erotic imagery of the poems has been allegorized by Sufis to enhance their mystical union. They decode the sensual language and find spiritual meaning. The "tavern" was a meeting place for a group of dervishes who drink wine ("remember" God) and the Beloved is God Himself. Glassé says Fitzgerald "crammed [the *Rubaiyat*] as full of Sufi love as only a nineteenth-century Victorian orientalist could."[28]

Prose

ARABIAN NIGHTS

This book, otherwise called *A Thousand and One Nights*, is a collection of stories about urban life in ninth- and tenth-century Basra, Cairo, and Baghdad.

These erotic and spiritual tales, many of them borrowed from Arab legends, Egyptian love stories, and Indian fairy tales, are really a political statement. The heroine is Shahrazad, who marries a wicked king known for his love of stories and women. After a woman tells a story, she is put to death. Shahrazad therefore never completes a story in one evening, but finishes it and immediately begins another on the next evening. In the process, she bears him three children, and after a thousand and one nights is rewarded for her stories with her life. The strong sense of fairness and the righting of wrong in these tales appealed to Islam's passion for justice and reinforced its concern for the ill-treatment of women.

Philosophy

Being a culture whose primary basis of authority was Revelation, philosophy as such was not important in early Muslim thought. There were theologians or at best philosophers of religion. So, much of Islamic philosophy in the Golden Age was an amalgam of Indian and Hellenistic thought. Once Platonism, Aristotelianism, and Hinduism began to infiltrate Islamic theology, there was a move away from the centrality of Revelation as the only way of knowing about the Divine. Beginning with al-Kindi (d. 873), the first to translate Aristotle into Arabic, and with al-Farabi (d. 956), who was very much influenced by Neo-Platonism, Islamic theologians used their reason (something the Quran celebrated as God's gift) to buttress religious belief. The Mutazilites were an eventual product of this cultural impact.

The union of faith and reason is not accidental because, as we have seen, philosophy and mathematics were often combined in Muslim scholarship. The concern to think clearly and logically is inherent in both disciplines.

Abu Ali al Husayn ibn Sina (d. 1037), known as Avicenna in the West, was a good example of the scholar who fused philosophy and science. For his time Avicenna was a maverick thinker, giving too much credence to philosophy as a way of understanding God. He really was a philosopher of religion who believed reason was able to prove God's existence and legitimize religious doctrine. Avicenna was so threatening to main line orthodoxy that Al-Ghazali, championing Revelation as the primary source of knowledge about God, wrote his attack on philosophy with Avicenna in mind.

Besides philosophy, Avicenna was considered an authority on medicine, and his medical manuals were used well into seventeenth-century Europe.

Abul Ibn Rushd (d. 1198). The most influential of all the Golden Age philosophers was this brilliant Cordova-born Muslim known as Averroes to the historians of western philosophy. He, too, was a multi-faceted intellectual with profound knowledge of mathematics and medicine who could split philosophical hairs with the best of his contemporaries.

Averroes was acquainted with the thought of Plato and Aristotle, but he was an expert in the latter's logic and metaphysics. He could advocate it so well that he was known as the "Islamic Aristotelian." He read all of Aristotle he could find and eventually wrote such a scholarly commentary on the Greek thinker's work that it became a standard source, and Averroes, himself, was called the "Second Master."

His loyalty to reason as a tool for understanding reality was accompanied by disdain for the masses' ability to use rational means to comprehend spiritual truth. While he understood the place of intuition, he much preferred the power of rational and philosophical debate. He was thought in some circles to be a heretic with his "Two Truth Theory"—one truth for the people (religion) and one truth for the enlightened (philosophy). But since Revelation (*Wahy*) still had priority for Averroes, he was not condemned. His later refutation of Al-Ghazali's refutation of Avicenna revealed him as a moderating voice; he saw no direct conflict between philosophy and religion.

Dante was so impressed with Averroes as the "Great Commentator" on Aristotle that he placed him, along with Avicenna, in Limbo, the first circle of Hell. "While these intellectual giants of Islam, along with the Roman poet Virgil, remain in this circle, it is, as someone has said, 'the easiest room in hell.' " This is not so much a compliment to Dante as it is a tribute to those philosophers who were true to their Islamic heritage of uniting faith and reason. Furthermore, it is generally agreed that Dante's journey to Heaven (Paradise) was modeled on Muhammad's "Night Journey."

Christians owe a tremendous debt to Averroes for preserving the work of Aristotle. It is highly unlikely that Thomas Aquinas could have written his defense of the Christian faith in *Summa Theologica* without the careful scholarship of this Muslim philosopher.

Sir Hamilton Gibb, a well-known early twentieth-century orientalist, theorized that a culture will absorb the content of another culture until its very center is threatened. The heart of Islam, namely its religion, was finally so threatening to Christian Europe that Islam was dismissed by the West. But many "non-religious" accomplishments of Islamic culture were assimilated by western leaders and scholars.

The modern tension between the West and the Islamic Arab world might be ameliorated by acknowledging the debt we owe to the thriving progressive civilization of Islam of a thousand years ago.

Part Five
Islam and Christianity

Jesus, Son of Mary

One of the first questions Christians want to ask Muslims is, "What do you think of Jesus?" Well, Islam thinks very highly of Jesus, more highly than any other religion save Christianity. The Quran assigns Jesus such titles as "Messenger," "Messiah," "Prophet," "Son of Mary," "Word of God," "Sign," and "Servant." There are at least thirty-five references to Jesus (*Isa*) and dozens of other verses in which Jesus is called by other names and titles. Suras 2-5 contain most of them.

Jesus is considered the most significant Prophet (Rasul) next to Muhammad. A cardinal tenet of Islam's faith is belief in Jesus; you cannot be a Muslim without honoring Jesus as a revelation from God. P.B.U.H. (Peace Be Unto Him) follows every mention of Jesus' name by a devout Muslim.

How do Muslims understand Jesus?

Virgin Birth

The stories of Jesus' birth in the Quran (3:42-44, 19:16-40) are rather similar to the account in the Gospel of Luke. About one-half of Sura 19 (approximately forty-five verses) discusses the role of Mary. There is no question about the

importance of Mary and her virginity. Indeed, some non-Muslims have remarked that there is more about Mary in the
Quran than in the New Testament.

After beginning with a record of the birth of John the Baptist, Sura 19 moves to the angelic visitation (Annunciation) and the birth of Jesus. These are followed by some comments on the meaning of Jesus for Islam. Sura 3 is a briefer version of the same story.

According to the Quran, God sent an angel to inform Mary she was to be the mother of the Holy Prophet Jesus. Her reply was similar to the Biblical Mary's: "How can I have a child? No man has touched me, and I am not unchaste." (19:20). The angel replied, "The Lord says: 'That will be easy for me; and We wish to appoint him as a Sign unto men and a Mercy from Us.' " (19:21)

Mary believed the angel, conceived, and eventually gave birth to her Son under a palm tree. Though Jesus was born of a Virgin, Islam does not believe that He is divine or the Son of God. That kind of association with God would be a violation of Tawhid. Just as the first prophet, Adam, was created by fiat, Jesus was conceived by the Word of God. Allah says to Mary: "Be" and "it is." (19:35) Furthermore Islam does not believe that Jesus needed to be divine to perform miracles. The Quran happily recounts his miracles and reminds us that God helped the prophet Moses perform several miracles.

While her son was quite young, Mary presented him to the villagers. They were amazed at his capacity for language when he said, "I am indeed a servant of God; He hath given me Revelation and made me a Prophet." (19:30)

In Islam the Virgin Birth of Jesus has less to do with Jesus than with the power of God and the Islam (submission) of Mary. His birth does not guarantee him any superiority among the prophets nor make him the Son of God. The Quran is careful in every instance to call him the Son of Mary. Islam allows that Jesus may be a son of God in the metaphorical sense as each of us may be if we obey and believe in One God.

Mary, the mother of Jesus, is the only woman in the Quran called by her proper name. This indicates in what high regard she is held by the Quran and how highly esteemed she is in Islam. All other women in the Quran are identified by relationship to a man. This regard for Mary, however, does not issue in any veneration of her, as in Christian Catholicism.

Jesus and the Gospel

According to Islam, Jesus came, as prophets before him, with a divine message. This message was the Gospel (*Injil*—Arabic for Evangel or Good News). The Gospel here is not to be confused with the four gospels although the latter may retain aspects of the Injil.

There are some specific meanings to Gospel in Islam. The Gospel is not the life of Jesus, but the message Jesus brought from Allah, namely a confirmation of Abraham's monotheism and Moses' revelation of Torah, which was the original true religion of God. Furthermore, as a confirming revelation from Allah, the Gospel refers to Jesus' prophethood, his Islam (submission to God), and his stress that the spirit of the law should take precedence over its letter. S. S. Mufassir sums up Islam's view of the Gospel this way: "The Good News which Jesus brought—the Gospel or Injil—was a renewal and affirmation of God's revelation to Moses, a message reaffirming God's love, mercy, justice and guidelines for living to those who would keep His covenant."[29] The Quranic summary is in Sura 5:67-72.

You might say that Islam sees as authentic the religion *of* Jesus and is inspired by that, not the churches' and subsequent first-century religion *about* Jesus.

Crucifixion

It is commonly held by Muslims that Jesus did not die on the cross, but was taken up into heaven by God before his death. The operative verses are 4:157-159. The context of these verses is a strong polemic against the Jews for "straying from the guidance of the Book" and in particular for falsely charging Mary with unchastity. Then, the Jews go on to boast, as the Quran says, "We killed Christ Jesus the Son of Mary, the Apostle of God." Then a quick caveat is added: "But they killed him not, nor crucified him; but it was made to appear to them. For of a surety they killed him not. Nay, God raised him up into Himself."

These verses have been subjected to a great deal of examination and varying interpretation. Do they mean Jesus died bodily and his spirit lives? Did Jesus only appear to die as early Christian docetists claimed? Did the Jews kill his body, but not his message? Some first- and second-century interpreters theorized that a substitute was made for Jesus at the last minute. Goeffrey Parrinder, in his *Jesus in the Quran,* traces in some detail the argument for and against the "substitute theory" and its sources in Christian and Muslim literature.[30] It is very clear, however, that neither scripture, the New Testament or the Quran, mentions a substitute.

H. Abdalati presents a convincing Islamic argument for Islam's denial of the death of Jesus in his *Islam in Focus.*[31] Chief among his theses are: (1) Can the crucifixion be reconciled with the justice, mercy, power, and wisdom of God? (2) Is Jesus' death at the hands of his enemies consistent with the providence of God? (3) Is it feasible to believe that the God who forgave Adam and Eve their sin would need a sacrifice of Jesus to forgive the human race?

The last argument is the most compelling from an Islamic perspective. The death of Jesus is of little interest to the Quran because Islam is not really interested in atonement for sin. While for Christians the death of Jesus is an incontrovertible historical fact and theologically indispensable, for

Islam its historicity is problematical, and Jesus' death, at best, is theologically confusing.* Perhaps the conclusion of the Muslim-Christian Research Group says it best: "The two religions consider that the end of Jesus' life on earth was 'extraordinary' and that God took him up, whether after his death and resurrection [for Christians] or without death and crucifixion [for Muslims]."[32]

Jesus the Prophet

Jesus, as we have mentioned, is called many names in the Quran: Apostle, Messenger, Messiah, Word, and Prophet. The Quran does not present discreet definitions or draw neat distinctions among them; that is why there is a good deal of overlap in their usage. However, it would be helpful for Christians to be aware of the Islamic version of these titles.

Jesus is a Word from God with the message of Islam, not the Eternal Logos of John's Gospel. Jesus as Messiah means Jesus the Messenger. Jesus the Apostle is also Jesus the Prophet. It is the latter title by which Jesus is best known in the Quran and for which he is honored by Muslims. Although "prophet" is the grandest title a human being can be assigned, he is still human. Sura 4:171 is an example of how many titles for Jesus can be found in a verse and yet be crystal clear about Jesus' humanity: "Christ Jesus the Son of Mary was no more than an Apostle of God and His Word,

---

*See the extensive bibliography on this subject in a footnote on p. 99 in *Challenge of the Scriptures: The Bible and the Quran* by Muslim-Christian Research Group (Maryknoll, NY: Orbis Books, 1989).

which He bestowed on Mary, and a Spirit proceeding from Him." (see also 5:78)

S. S. Mufassir has paraphrased 3:45-53 to give us a complete picture of Jesus in the Quran: "The Quran verifies that the Gospel of Jesus describes him as a Word from God, the Messiah, born of the Virgin Mary, a prophet and messenger of God to the people of Israel who relieved them of the restrictive, man-made additions to the Torah and who performed many miracles by God's permission, including healing the blind, curing diverse diseases and raising the dead, and that he taught the Oneness of God, whom he called his Lord."[33]

For the average Muslim Jesus is an example of sanctity and piety and someone who embodied true Islam. For this reason he is accorded more honor and deference than all the prophets who preceded Muhammad.

Bases for Dialogue

There are two Suras which are virtual invitations to dialogue:

 Say, O People of the Book! Come to common terms
 as between me and you. That we worship none but
 God, that we associate no partners with Him, that we
 erect not from ourselves Lords and Patrons other
 than God. (3:66)

 Invite all to the Way of thy Lord with wisdom and
 beautiful preaching, and argue with them in ways
 that are best and most gracious. (16:125)

Let us attempt to see what "common terms" there are between Christianity and Islam and try to do so in ways that
are "best and most gracious." This will be at the same time
both easy and difficult. Our attempt to find "common
ground" will be difficult because we both make absolute
claims and appear to hold uncompromising convictions
about the nature of God. But our task will be easy because
both religions are solidly within the Abrahamic/Jewish tradition and cannot be understood apart from that tradition. We
belong to no other family of religions. In addition, from the
time of Muhammad, Islam has been less critical of Christianity than of Judaism and far more expansive toward Jesus

than any other religious figure. That is an important positive note to strike at the beginning.

We will need much grace to speak of our differences. We may feel tremors beneath our common ground as we engage in dialogues about some fundamental points which divide us. Both Christianity and Islam are triumphalist, absolutist, missionary-oriented religions. Both insist each is the true religion. What would a dialogue look like in the framework of two apparently mutually exclusive religious claims: "There is no God but God and Muhammad is the Prophet of God" and the words of Jesus: "I am the Way, the Truth, and the Life; no one comes to the Father but by me." Let us explore some possibilities.

A framework for honest dialogue should include a statement of similarities and differences between Islam and Christianity. Throughout this book I have suggested comparisons and contrasts between the two religions. Now I would like to do so in a more systematic way.

Differences

1. Christianity and Islam differ on which family tree fulfilled most adequately the promises made to Abraham. Was it the family of Isaac or the family of Ishmael? Christians say the promise to Isaac ended with Jesus who was the fulfillment of all Old Testament prophesy. Islam claims that Muhammad was the fulfilling Prophet of Ishmael's tradition.

2. Both religions differ on the nature of human beings. Christianity, on the whole, has a negative view of human nature and asserts that we are fallen creatures. Therefore, the doctrine of original sin is a central category for Christians. We are saved only by the death and resurrection of Christ. Islam has a more positive notion of men and women and does not believe we are lost persons. Hence, it rejects the theology which supports original sin. We are "saved" by following the guidance provided for us in the Quran.

3. These differing views of human nature naturally lead to differing views about Jesus. What Christians see as the heart and soul of their faith—the divine Sonship of Jesus, his Incarnation, Crucifixion, Resurrection, and the Trinity—are seen by Islam as distortions and alterations of true Islam, the original revelation of God. It is instructive to recall some verses from the Quran to understand Islam's point of view:

> They do blaspheme who say "God is Christ the Son of Mary." But said Christ: "O Children of Israel! Worship God, my Lord and your Lord." Whoever joins other gods with God, God will forbid him the Garden and the Fire will be his abode. (5:75 and see also 5:19)

> And behold! God will say: "O Jesus Son of Mary! Didst thou say unto people, worship me and my mother as gods in derogation of God?" He [Jesus] will say: "Glory to Thee." Never would I say what I had no right to say. (5:119)

It is also clear from these statements that Mary is not to be venerated or worshiped in any way.

4. For 300 years now, Christianity generally has divided the political and ecclesiastical realms. Christians have accommodated themselves to the separation of church and state and have not required a religious test for leadership of a nation. Islam, on the other hand, legislates for all aspects of life and for all its followers, including political leaders.

5. Christianity underwent the critique of the European Enlightenment—that confrontation with rational, romantic, and revolutionary philosophy which has indelibly engraved upon Western consciousness the marks of individual freedom, ideological tolerance, and self-criticism. It also secularized our values to a point almost incomprehensible to Muslims. Islam has never experienced a similar time when ultimate

values were so relativized. Since Islam's inception, reason and faith have had a close, if sometimes stormy, relationship.

Dialogue presupposes that each side wishes to know the other, and wishes to increase and deepen its knowledge of the other. It constitutes a particularly suitable means of favoring a better mutual knowledge and...of probing the riches of one's own tradition. Dialogue demands respect for the other as he is; above all, respect for his faith and his religious convictions.

Vatican Guidelines, 1975

Similarities

Although there are differences, some might say irreconcilable differences, between Christianity and Islam, there are many similarities that we do well to emphasize. The Second Vatican Council highlighted these common elements twenty-five years ago in one of its documents, *Nostra Aetate*:

> The Church also has a high regard for the Muslims. They worship God, who is one, living and subsistent, merciful and almighty, the Creator of heaven and earth, who has also spoken to men. They strive to submit themselves without reserve to the hidden decrees of God, just as Abraham submitted himself to God's plan, to whose faith Muslims eagerly link their own. Although not acknowledging him as God, they venerate Jesus as a prophet, his virgin Mother they also honor, and even at times devoutly invoke. Further, they await the day of judgment and the rewards of God following the resurrection of the dead. For this reason they highly esteem an upright life and worship God, especially by way of prayer, alms-deeds and fasting.

1. There is a joint legacy of a Biblical tradition and the same heritage of prophethood. Both Christianity and Islam come

from Judaism, share the common parentage of Abraham, and delight in the Jewish Torah.

2. Islam and Christianity are both monotheistic religions and ascribe similar attributes to God: Creator, Sustainer, Judge, Merciful, Forgiver. God and Allah both act in history to further causes of justice, peace, and harmony among all people.

3. Both religions are universal in scope, claiming to transcend differences of race, ethnicity, nationality, and color.

4. Christianity and Islam are both committed to praxis: a unification of faith and life, prayer and action. They are strongly ethical religions. The Christian unity of grace and law is similar to the unity of mercy and Shariah in Islam.

5. Both faiths make absolute claims to perfect truth about God. In this way, they resemble most religions founded on divine revelation. As a result, when they speak, they are certain they are speaking in the name of that Absolute.

6. Christianity and Islam both say they purify and fulfill religions that preceded them: Christianity for Judaism, Islam for both Judaism and Christianity.

7. Both religions believe that history has a goal and will culminate in the return of Christ and the Mahdi, both Messianic figures at the last day. Accompanying this is a common belief in Last Judgment, the Resurrection and an after-life in Heaven (Garden) or Hell (Fire).

8. Islam and Christianity emphasize personal acts of piety such as prayer, fasting, charity, and scripture reading. They share as well the prophetic call to help the oppressed, the poor, the widow, the orphan, and the homeless.

9. Christianity and Islam are growing, dynamic religions with progressive, reactionary, and mainstream dimensions in both of them. And in each case, change is not betraying the core of the respective faith.

10. Both exemplify the human tendency to fall short of the ideals of their founders and scriptures. Christians fail to live up to the model of Jesus, and Muslims seldom achieve the standards set by the Quran. We are united in human frailty, but more importantly in the human aspiration to be the best Muslim or Christian we can be. All these points of unity and agreement should be emphasized as a basis for dialogue.

A concrete way to illustrate our similarities and differences is to see how Islam responds to a common denominator of Christian faith, the Apostles Creed. A. Guillaume suggested this in his book entitled *Islam*.[34] The words in italics are the beliefs rejected by Islam.

I believe in God, *the Father* Almighty,
Maker of heaven and earth.
And in Jesus Christ *His only Son, our Lord*
Who was conceived by the Holy Ghost,
Born of the Virgin Mary

Suffered under Pontius Pilate, Was crucified,
Dead? *and buried. He descended into hell;*
The third day He rose again from the dead.
He ascended into heaven,
And sitteth on the right hand of God
the Father Almighty;
From thence He shall come
to judge the quick and the dead.
I believe in the Holy Spirit;
The Holy Catholic Church;
The Communion of Saints;
The forgiveness of sins;
The Resurrection of the body,
and the life everlasting.

All the italicized differences have been addressed in one form or another in this *Primer*, but a bit more might be said about the death of Jesus.

There is explicit denial of Jesus' crucifixion in the Quran, but some other passages speak of his death: "So peace is on me the day I was born, the day that I die, and the day I shall be raised up to life again." (19:33) There may be a distinction here between Jesus' death and the mode of his death, namely crucifixion, or this verse and 3:55 are saying that Allah took the soul of Jesus the way he took other figures, such as Enoch, unto Himself. It is safe to conclude that the majority of Muslims believe the latter.

Admittedly, this concrete example of the Creed has to do with belief and theology. At the level of ethical concerns, there would be very little difference. I am mindful of a statement al-Faruqi made several years ago: "In the circumstances in which Muslim and Christians find themselves today, primacy belongs to the ethical questions, not the theological."[35]

What Christians Can Do
To Better Understand Islam

The following list of concepts, if considered by Christians, could further the understanding of Islam:

1. That Islam is not a new religion, but a renewal and restoration of the religion of Jesus, Moses, and Abraham—the original religion God planned for everyone.

2. The Muslim pain of having been the butt of centuries of Christian slander, misrepresentation, and ridicule. Dante, Luther, and nineteenth-century European missionaries and colonizers helped fuel this devaluation.

3. That no other religion in the world, until the Bahais, has made acceptance of the truths of other religions conditions for its membership. (5:71)

4. How and why Islam was so offended by Salman Rushdie's *Satanic Verses*. It cannot be reduced to a "free speech" issue. Muslims feel his book was the most profound of blasphemous and scandalous acts.

Hans Kung, a Roman Catholic theologian who has studied Islam for many years, suggests three other ways Christians can attempt to increase their understanding of Islam:

5. See Islam as a path of salvation, indeed, the closest to ours as any other world religion.

6. View Muhammad as an authentic prophet of God.

7. Understand the Quran as a revealed scripture, not a mixture of Arab, Jewish, Christian, and Hellenistic religions.

What Muslims Can Do
To Better Understand Christianity

The following list of concepts, if considered by Muslims, could further the understanding of Christianity:

1. A fundamental estrangement and separation of men and women from God, each other, and nature (what Christians call original sin).

2. The correlative Christian emphasis on atonement and reconciliation as benefits of the Crucifixion of Christ.

3. Christianity as an intact religion and a path of salvation.

4. That Jesus, being the divine Son of God, was more than a prophet and that the Gospel was an historical act of God's mercy.

5. That Christianity does not see monotheism and its belief in the Trinity as mutually exclusive.

6. That for most Christians, works (good deeds) are a product of God's grace, not a condition for receiving it.

To be sure, for Christians and Muslims to attempt to walk in each other's shoes at these critical points means risk and a good deal of discomfort, but this honest uneasiness could create a healthy tension for authentic dialogue.

Guidelines for Dialogue

Leonard Swidler, Professor of Catholic Thought and Inter-religious Dialogue at Temple University, has come up with an extremely helpful set of guidelines for interreligious/intercultural dialogue. These suggestions came out of Swidler's own theoretical work and his practical experience. They furnish sensible and sensitive guidance for any group interested in dialogue.

He calls these guidelines *The Dialogue Decalogue*.[36]

1. The primary purpose of dialogue is to learn, that is, to change and grow in the perception and understanding of reality and then to act accordingly. We enter into dialogue not to convert another (that is preaching) or to win arguments (that is debating). But the willingness to listen and to learn and be ready to revise previously held opinions is a predication of dialogue.

2. Interreligious dialogue must be a two-sided project— within each religious community and between religious communities. Dialogue should take place at the *inter*religious level, that is, between Muslims and Christians and also at the *intra*religious level, that is, among Christians so that the benefits of dialogue at the ecumenical stage can be realized at the parish level.

3. *Each participant must come to the dialogue with complete honesty and sincerity...and, conversely, each participant must assume a similar complete honesty and sincerity in the other partners.* There is to be no hidden agenda or "false fronts."

4. *In interreligious dialogue we must not compare our ideals with our partner's practice, but rather our ideals with our partner's ideals, our practice with our partner's practice.* This is the pit into which much interreligious dialogue falls. We tend to compare our best with their worst, our perfection with the other's mistakes, our strength with our partner's weakness, our sufficiency with their deficiency. This is patently unfair and constitutes, as Islam would say, not weighing with even scales.

5. *Participants must be allowed to define themselves and conversely, the one interpreted must be able to recognize himself or herself in the interpretation.* Swidler calls this the golden rule of dialogue.

6. *Each participant must come to the dialogue with no hard and fast assumptions as to where the points of disagreement are.* This is a form of pre-judgment which prejudices the conversations and may prevent openness for a new understanding and agreement when it occurs.

7. Dialogue can take place only between equals. If Christians feel superior to Muslims, dialogue is impossible. Equality in dialogue also means that an imam would converse with a clergy of some denomination and not with a layperson and vice versa.

8. Dialogue can take place only on the basis of mutual trust. Mutual respect and trust are indispensable. Christian-Muslim dialogue, for instance, cannot be seen by the Muslim as another form of Christian-Western hegemony or the satisfaction of a missionary impulse.

9. Persons entering into interreligious dialogue must be at least minimally self-critical of both themselves and their own religious or ideological traditions. True dialogue is not possible if one side feels it is above criticism or has a corner on the Truth. Absolute truth is hardly known absolutely. Mutually exclusive claims cancel out each other. In dialogue we can discover the nature of the partner's claims and why he or she makes them. Having said all this, true dialogue also insists that we each maintain our religious integrity and deeply held convictions.

10. Each participant eventually must attempt to experience the partner's religion or ideology "from within." Empathy contributes immensely to dialogue because religion, as both St. Francis and al-Ghazali taught us, is a unity of the cognitive and the affective, the head and the heart. To feel each other's "heart" is a sure way to understanding.

What we have discussed is dialogue, not monologue, debate, or much less what Faruqi called "diatribe." Through dialogue we attempt to become aware, to understand, to learn.

I hasten to say that dialogue does not diminish differences. Understanding does not mean agreement or the blurring of distinction between religious claims. It is precisely those differences, honestly admitted and squarely faced, which might become the midwife of new knowledge. Without having to convert or to change someone's mind, we may achieve, in the words of a group of Muslims and Christians after a series of dialogues, "respect for the irreconcilable." That respect and candor maintains our integrity and allows us to live peaceably together.

I have learned and re-learned a great deal from talking with and listening to Muslims. Here is a brief list:

That religion has to do with all of life;

That attitudes toward God and religious speech should be taken with ultimate seriousness;

That prayer is central to religious life;

That my post-Enlightenment Christianity leans more to tolerance than to conviction; and

That we in the West may want to think of re-sacralizing our secularized values to which we may have grown too accustomed.

It is fitting to conclude this chapter on the possibility for Muslim-Christian dialogue with two statements from Muslims. Yusuf Ali in his commentary on Sura 16:125, a verse with which this chapter begins, says:

Our manner and our arguments should not be acrimonious, but modelled on the most courteous and the most gracious example, so that the hearer may say to himself, "This man is not dealing merely with dialectics; he is not trying to get a rise out of me; he is sincerely expounding the faith that is in him, and his motive is the love of man and the love of God."

The other hopeful statement is from Sheikh Ahmad Kuftaro, Grand Mufti of Syria, who said, "We can appreciate the role of faith in God as being the most vigorous and active factor governing human behavior; for it urges human beings to unite, to cooperate, to love one another, to do away with all sorts of discrimination, racial, color, or tribal, and to congregate under God's command."[37]

Concluding Reflections

The Heart of Islam:
Continuity, Certainty, and Balance

As a Christian, I obviously cannot speak about Islam "from within." As empathetic as I might try to be, I am still an outsider. However, after my study, research, and an earnest attempt to feel the Muslim pulse, I have some final thoughts about the spirit of Islam.

I have intentionally chosen the metaphor of "heart" because for Islam the "heart" is the center of our being. What is the center of Islam's being? F. Schuon, in his little book, *Understanding Islam,*[38] suggests two central categories that I have borrowed: "equilibrium" and "certitude." I have added the third category of continuity. Actually, all three categories, in one form or the other, are found in the Quran, and almost all Muslim scholars have had to deal with these "essences" of Islam. The most recent and well-known are al-Faruqi and F. Rahman.

Continuity

As we have repeatedly noted, Islam sees itself as the fulfillment of the Jewish and Christian religions, its Quran as the
apogee of Scriptures (Torah and Gospel), and its Prophet
Muhammad as the Seal of all Prophethood from Jesus back
to Adam. Islam completed the religion of Jesus, which
Christians believe completed Jewish religion. This link of
"fulfillment" of Biblical religion, scripture, and prophets is
one illustration of continuity.

Another way of saying this is that Islam asserts there has
been only one Revelation and only one religion; that is
Islam. It is not the youngest religion, but in fact, the oldest.
It started in Eden when Adam and Eve said a form of the
Shahadah as they witnessed to the Oneness and Unity of
Allah (7:172). Since that time, a certain number of prophets
have received a succession of Revelations from God. So
when the final Prophet Muhammad received his Revelation,
it was a return—back beyond Gospel and Torah, back beyond such Muslims as Jesus, Moses, and Abraham, to
Adam. This link of "return" to an original purity is another
example of continuity.

An architectural symbol of Islam's vocation of fulfillment is
the Dome of the Rock which is built on the Temple Mount in
Jerusalem. This "Mount," Jews claim, has been the location
of the First and Second Temples, sacred sites of Judaism.

The continuity is not just longitudinal; it is latitudinal as well. A Hadith says that every child born is born a Muslim with the natural inclination to Islam. We are not original sinners; we are original Muslims. Even the great al-Ghazali implied as much when he quoted the saying of the Prophet, "Everyone who is born is born with a sound nature; it is his parents who make him a Jew or a Christian or a Magian."[39] All humankind is organically connected by the thread of Islam.

Another example of latitudinal continuity is that Islam is not a religion which compartmentalizes life; it is a total way of life. Like Allah's mercy, it comprehends every aspect of our existence from government to law to social relations to economics to religion. All of life's dimensions are viewed as a seamless garment, very much like the pilgrim's ritual garment for Hajj. The link of brotherhood and sisterhood is a further illustration of continuity.

Certainty

The sources of Islam's absolute assurance of its validity lie in reason and revelation. Muslims can trust human reason because the intellect is one of the main gifts bestowed upon human beings at Creation. As a consequence Muslims feel that the truth of Islam is discoverable and verifiable by common sense and reasonableness.

The Islamic concept of Reason is similar to the Western notion of Natural Law which has been a reliable and authoritative guide for theology and ethics. Muslim scholars have confounded many non-Muslims by their irrefutable logic and the internal coherence of their arguments. Islam's case for Tawhid and monotheism is a clear example of their rationality at work.

The other source of certainty is the Quran, God's definitive scriptural text. One of the most important Suras begins, "There is no doubt in this Book." (2:2) Not only is the content of the Quran without doubt; its very creation is beyond doubt. It is, as the Muslims say, a "Standing Miracle" or a "literary marvel." What could have been its origin except God? If the Quran is the direct speech of God, it is invested with ultimate sanctity and therefore certainty is assured.

If non-Muslims wonder why Islam accepts the Quran as absolute, it is because the Quran says it is absolute. Muslims look no further for an "objective" or "externally based" criterion for proof. The truth of the Quran is self-validating. Islamic logic begins with this premise. The Quran, as the Word of God, is free from error because God is not subject to error. Muslims who follow the Quran, then, feel they are as free from error as one can be on this earth.

It would be a mistake to call this blind faith. All the Muslim scholars I have referred to agree on these assumptions about the Quran. They find the words of their scriptures as self-evidently true as Americans find the truths of the Declaration of Independence self-evident and as many Christians find the truths of the Bible verified by II Timothy 3:16, "All scripture is inspired by God...." In each case, no further documentation is needed.

Perhaps from a historical point of view, it was the heritage of the fragility of desert life and the need to migrate regularly for survival which gave rise to the importance of certainty in Muslim religious life. "Journey" was a basic metaphor for the Arab's existence. "Living on the edge" from day to day created doubt and guaranteed the relativity of life. The shift from an unpredictable hand of Fate to the unshakeable mercy of an absolute God was abetted by the certainty of the Quran.

One can now understand the utter loyalty Muslims have for the Quran, their undying allegiance to Allah, and the uncritical confidence in the "rightness" of their religion. Schuon intimates that if Christianity is the religion of the love of God, then Islam is the religion of the Absolute God.

Balance

One of the key images in Islam is "evenly balanced scales." As we mentioned earlier this image is undoubtedly rooted in the merchant life of Mecca and other cities in Arabia. Sura 55:7-9 reflects this demand for "balance":

And the Firmament has He raised high, and He has set up the Balance of justice in order that you may not transgress due to balance. So establish weight with justice and fall not short in the balance. (See also 17:35 and 83: 1-6.)

This may be, after all, one of Islam's greatest contributions to Western religious and cultural understanding. Sura 2:143 calls Islam a "just nation," or a "middle nation" as some translators put it. Islam, as a religion which mediates between extremes, pleads for the Golden Mean, for equitable and realistic moderation. It believes that life is healthier when tension is not exacerbated and harmonious balance is maintained. The Buddhist "Middle Way" and Hegel's "synthesis of opposites" are other expressions which remind humanity to avoid extremes.

There are countless ways Islam illustrates its impulse for equilibrium and balance. For example, the Quran emphasizes the unity of the individual's contribution to society and in turn the society's responsibility to protect the individual; it condemns both self-pity (despair) and self-righteousness (pride); it is concerned that sexual desires not be promiscuously satisfied or puritanically repressed; it is clear that Allah is both merciful and just; if the Jews rejected Jesus and if Christians thought him a God, Islam finds a balance in his exceptional prophethood.

The Quran seeks an appropriate and practical balance between free will and predestination, Revelation and reason, this world and the next, faith and works, and human egoism and altruism.

Muhammad's life and teaching are examples of the "middle way." He effectively combined the spiritual and the ethical, the ascetic and the worldly, family life and community duties. Al-Faruqi recalls a story which exemplifies Muhammad's inclination to balance: "When asked if a person should pray all night and fast all year, the Prophet said, 'God did not provide it. As for me, I pray and I sleep. I fast and I eat. I work and I keep women company.' " Muhammad was not a libertine or an ascetic. He moderated the spiritual and the physical the way a tenth-century "brother of purity" Ikhwan al-Safa balanced his understanding of life: "food for the body and knowledge for the soul."

In addition, the Hadith and generations of Muslim scholars, using the model of equilibrium, sought a via media between:

— capitalism and socialism

— the absolute ideals of the Quran and the flexible application of the Shariah to the realities of life

— complementary roles of wife and husband

— Sufi love and Islamic knowledge

— marriage as neither sacrament nor civil contract, but a personal covenant

— rights and duties of being a Muslim

All of this confirms that Islam is aware of and sensitive to the whole gamut of human desires and needs—physical, emotional, spiritual, and intellectual. All these needs and desires are from God and, within boundaries, should be enjoyed.

The architectural symbol of Islam's equilibrium is the Kaaba. It balances, integrates, and centers the Muslim world. At the Kaaba priority is not ascribed to any extreme, no side outweighs the other.

AFTERWORD

This has been an exercise in understanding, an attempt to appreciate what, why, and how Muslims believe and act the way they do. My original concern seems to have been borne out; the more Christians understand Islam, the less intimidating and threatening Islam becomes. Or to put it positively, an objective look at what Islam really is will give us access to one of the world's richest and most vital religious traditions, access that has heretofore been denied us by our centuries-long legacy of suspicion and ignorance.

The more Christians get to know Muslims, the more Christians will see themselves in Islam and the less strange Islam will become. The reverse, of course, is also true. My challenge to the reader is that in future dialogues Christians and Muslims always compare the best of one faith with the best in the other.

Christianity and Islam will continue to grow and will be for the foreseeable future the two largest religions in the world. How will we manage our life together? The road may not be easy, but I firmly believe it is passable. If we can balance successfully our inclusive *and* exclusive claims, we will mutually enrich each other's faith and the world will be a better place.

Appendices

Islam's Calendar

MONTHS IN THE LUNAR YEAR

1. Muharra
2. Safar
3. Rabi al-Awwai
4. Rabi ath-Thani
5. Jumada-al-Ula
6. Jumada-al-akhira
7. Rajab
8. Shaban
9. Ramadan
10. Shawwai
11. Dhu al-Qadah
12. Dhu al-Hijjah

FESTIVALS

10th Muharra	Ashura: New Year's Celebration
12th Rabi-al-Awwai	Mawlid al-Nabi: Prophet's Birthday
27th Rajab	Laylat al-Miraj: The Night Journey
15th Shaban	Laylat al-Baraat: Night of Forgiveness
27th Ramadan	Laylat al-Qadr: The Night of Power
1st Shawwai	Id al-Fitr: Breaking Fast of Ramadan
Dhu al-Qadah	Preparation for Hajj
8th, 9th, 10th Dhu al-Hijjah	Hajj: Pilgrimage
10th Dhu al-Hijjah	Id al-Adha: Festival of Sacrifice (celebration of Abraham's readiness to sacrifice his son, Ishmael)

MAJOR ISLAMIC FESTIVALS

Ashura: The first month of Islam's calendar is the anniversary of Muhammad's "flight" to Medina. For Shiites, the 10th of this month is the sad remembrance of Husayn's death and during the first ten days of Muharran his death is recalled by a kind of passion play performed in Karbala.

Laylat al-Qadr: This celebration of the "Night of Power" is on one of the last ten nights of Ramadan. Many believe it is on the 27th night of the month. It commemorates the first appearance of the angel Gabriel to Muhammad and the beginning of the revelation of the Quran.

Laylat al-Miraj: This festival remembers Muhammad's Night Journey and Ascencion to Heaven and celebrates the institution of the Salat which the Prophet received that night. It also recognizes Islam's identity with Judaism and Christianity because on the night journey Muhammad met all the prophets who preceded him.

SOME CRUCIAL EVENTS IN ISLAMIC HISTORY

570 CE	Birth of Muhammad
610	Beginning of Quranic Revelation to Muhammad
622	Migration to Medina
630	Mecca is conquered by Muslim forces
632	Death of Muhammad
636–640	Islam expands to Damascus, Jerusalem, Egypt, and Persia
ca. 652	Quran canonized
680	Ali's son, Husayn, is murdered
711	Islam reaches Spain
713	Muslims enter eastern India
762	Baghdad founded
966	Cairo founded
1095	Christian Crusades begin
1099	Crusaders capture Jerusalem
1258	Mongols destroy Baghdad
1453	Ottoman takeover of Constantinople
1494	End of Muslim Spain
1730	Mogul rule in India effectively over
1924	Turkey becomes a secular state
1947	Creation of Pakistan

MOMENTS IN AMERICAN MUSLIM HISTORY

1539 Moroccan guide Estephan participated in the exploration of Arizona and New Mexico for the viceroy of New Spain

1717 Arrival in North America of "Arabic-speaking slaves who ate no pork and believed in Allah and Muhammad." 1790 "Moors" reported living in South Carolina

1856 Hajj Ali hired by the United States cavalry to experiment in raising camels in Arizona

1869 A number of Yemenis arrived after the opening of the Suez Canal

1900 Earliest recorded Muslim group to organize for communal prayer, in Ross, North Dakota

1913 Moorish-American Science Temple founded in Newark, New Jersey

1919 Islamic Association formed in Highland Park, Michigan

1922 Islamic Association formed in Detroit, Michigan

1930 Arab-American Banner Society formed in Quincy, Massachusetts

1930 Lost-Found Nation of Islam in the Wilderness of North America (Black Muslims) established

1934 First building designated as mosque, in Cedar Rapids, Iowa

1952 Muslim servicemen allowed to identify their religion as Muslim by the Federal government

1952 International Muslim Society (IMS) organized

1954 IMS renamed Federation of Islamic Associations (FIA)

1957 Islamic Center of Washington, D.C. opened

1963 Muslim Student's Association (MSA) founded

1972 Islamic Party of North America organized in Washington, D.C.

1974 Muslim World League granted non-governmental organization (NGO) status at the United Nations

1975 Warith Deen Muhammad renounced Elijah's teachings and restored the Nation of Islam to orthodoxy

1976 The Nation of Islam assumed the name of The World Community of Islam in the West as Warith Deen Muhammad began the reformation of the beliefs of the community

1977   First Islamic Conference of North America met in Newark. 1978 Warith Deen Muhammad named as consultant/trustee by Gulf States to distribute funds for Islamic missionary activities in U.S.

1980   The World Community of Islam in the West assumed the name of the American Muslim Mission

1981   The International Institute of Islamic Thought founded

1982   Islamic Society of North America (ISNA) formed

1983   Islamic College founded in Chicago

1985   Warith Deen Muhammad decentralized the American Muslim Mission

From "A Century of Islam in America" by Yvonne Haddad. *The Muslim World Today*, Occasional Paper No. 4, Middle East Institute, Washington, D.C. Used by permission.

ISLAMIC MOSQUES/CENTERS
IN THE UNITED STATES

	Muslim Student Association/ University Campuses	Mosques/ Centers Associations	Masjids of the American Muslim Mission	TOTAL
Alabama	1	2	10	13
Arkansas	1	1	1	3
Arizona	2	5	2	9
California	10	32	17	59
Colorado	3	3	2	8
Connecticut	–	5	5	10
Delaware	–	1	1	2
D.C.	–	8	1	9
Florida	4	10	7	21
Georgia	2	5	12	19
Hawaii	1	–	–	1
Idaho	1	–	–	1
Illinois	4	20	9	33
Indiana	5	8	7	20
Iowa	2	3	1	6
Kansas	2	3	3	8
Kentucky	–	2	2	4
Louisiana	–	3	4	7
Maine	1	–	–	1
Maryland	1	4	3	8
Massachusetts	5	12	4	21
Michigan	3	17	9	29
Minnesota	1	1	2	4
Mississippi	1	1	4	6
Missouri	2	3	2	7

	Muslim Student Association/ University Campuses	Mosques/ Centers Associations	Masjids of the American Muslim Mission	TOTAL
Nebraska	1	–	2	3
Nevada	1	–	1	2
New Hampshire	–	1	1	2
New Jersey	–	22	9	31
New Mexico	2	2	1	5
New York	7	61	14	82
North Carolina	3	7	8	18
North Dakota	2	–	–	2
Ohio	2	14	12	28
Oklahoma	1	3	3	7
Oregon	3	1	2	6
Pennsylvania	7	17	5	29
Rhode Island	–	2	1	3
South Carolina	–	1	7	8
Tennessee	2	1	4	7
Texas	7	8	11	26
Utah	1	–	–	1
Virginia	1	6	5	12
Washington	1	3	2	6
West Virginia	1	1	1	3
Wisconsin	3	3	2	8
TOTAL	**97**	**302**	**199**	**598**

Compiled from published lists by American Muslim Mission, Council of Masajid, Federation of Islamic Associations and the Muslim Student Association, as well as the newsletters of independent associations.

From "A Century of Islam in America" by Yvonne Haddad. *The Muslim World Today*, Occasional Paper No. 4, Middle East Institute, Washington, D.C. Used by permission.

SAMPLE LIST OF ENGLISH WORDS
DERIVED FROM ARABIC

admiral	divan
alcohol	elixir
alfalfa	nadir
algebra	sapphire
alkali	sherbet
arsenal	sugar
assassin	syrup
balcony	taffeta
borax	tariff
camphor	tobacco
candy	tulips
cipher	yoghurt
coffee	zenith

GLOSSARY OF ARABIC TERMS

Allah   The One and Only God

Aya   A verse of the Quran; literally, a "sign" of "miracle"—hence ayatollah is "mark of Allah"

Caliph   Successor to Muhammad, or one who rules a Muslim nation

dar al-Islam   Abode of Islam, or land where Islam is in majority

dar al-harb   Abode of War, or land where Islam is in a minority and where Muslims are persecuted

Dhikr   Remembrance or recollection; a Sufi meditation practice

Dhimmi   Non-Muslims who are "people of the Book," especially Jews and Christians, who live as protected minorities in an Islamic state

Dua   Spontaneous supplication as contrasted with prescribed prayers of Salat

Hadith   A report of a saying or activity of the Prophet

Hajj   Pilgrimage to Mecca; one of the Five Pillars of Islam

Hijra   (Hegira) Muhammad's flight or emigration from Mecca to Medina in 622. The Muslim calendar begins with this year.

Imam   In general, a leader of prayer; in particular, for Shiite Islam, a spiritual guide

Jihad   Struggle or striving in the name of Islam for a moral, spiritual, or political goal; one who struggles is a Mujtahid

Jinn   Invisible spirits referred to in Quran

Kaaba   Cube-shaped building in Mecca; the "Holy of Holies" for pilgrims and the place toward which all Muslim prayers are directed

Madrasa   A school designed for religious education, usually associated with a mosque

Mahdi   A messianic figure many Muslims believe will come at the end of time to establish a brief period of righteousness before the world ends

Masjid   Mosque; literally, a place of prostration

Mihrab   Arched niche in wall of mosque which is the *qibla* or direction of Mecca

Minbar	Pulpit from which sermons are preached at Friday noon prayers
Miraj	Muhammad's ascent to heaven or his famous "Night Journey"
Qibla	The direction of the Kaaba, toward which Muslims turn for their daily prayers
Quran	God's revelation to Muhammad; literally, Recitation; Islam's Scripture
Rakat	A unit of prayer which involves a Muslim's bodily action and verbal recitation
Ramadan	The month of fasting
Salam	Peace; also a greeting Muslims often exchange with each other
Salat	Literally, worship; used to denote prescribed, ritual prayer performed five times a day; one of the Five Pillars of Islam
Sawm	Fasting, usually associated with Ramadan; a Pillar of Islam
Shahadah	The affirmation or witness: "There is no God but God and Muhammad is the Prophet of God"; one of the Five Pillars of Islam

Shariah	Islamic law derived from the Quran and Muhammad's teaching and example
Sheikh	Literally, "mature" or "full of wisdom"; also a Sufi spiritual leader
Shiite	Muslims who are "Partisans" of Ali and who share his understanding of who should be the successor to the Prophet
Shirk	Associating any other reality with Allah, hence idolatry
Sufi	One who represents the mystical dimension of Islam; a Muslim who seeks direct experience of God
Sunna	The tradition and custom of Muhammad; second in authority only to the Quran
Sunni	One who follows the tradition of the Prophet
Takhir	Recitation of the phrase "Allahu Akbar" or "God is most Great"
Tariqa	Sufi path leading to direct knowledge of God; also a community or school of Sufism
Tawhid	The Divine Unity of God
Ulema	Learned scholars or religious specialists who are sought for the knowledge of Islamic law and teaching

Umma   The Muslim community

Wudu   Act of ritual ablution or purification by water before Salat

Zakat   Almsgiving for the poor; one of the Five Pillars of Islam

ENDNOTES

1. The only comparable effort is the excellent introduction by Marston Speight in *God is One: The Way of Islam* (New York: Friendship Press, 1989).

2. Bruce Lawrence, *Defenders of God: The Fundamentalist Revolt Against the Modern Age* (Harper and Row Publishers: San Francisco, 1989), pp. 194-195.

3. Bernard Lewis, *Baltimore Sunday Sun,* May 16, 1990.

4. Hammudah Abdalati, *Islam in Focus* (Delhi: Crescent Publishing Company, 1988), p. 105.

5. Sydney N. Fisher, *The Middle East: A History,* Second Edition (New York: Alfred A. Knopf, 1989), p. 23.

6. Muhammad H. Haykal, *The Life of Muhammad* (North American Trust Publications, 1976), p. 63.

7. Ibid., p. 100.

8. Letter to author, August 28, 1991.

9. Haykal, op. cit., p. xxiv.

10. Cyril Glassé, *A Concise Encyclopedia of Islam* (San Francisco: Harper and Row Publishers, 1989), p. 281.

11. See Abul-Ahad Dawud, *Muhammad and the Bible,* Second Edition (Kuala Lumpur: Pustaka Antara, 1979), p. 212; and Ulfat Azis-us-

Samad, *A Comparative Study of Christianity and Islam* (Farashkhana, Delhi, Noor Publishing House, 1986), p. 42.

12. Fazlur Rahman, *Major Themes of the Quran* (Minneapolis: Bibliotheca Islamica, 1989), p. 106.

13. Yusuf Qaradawi, *The Lawful and the Prohibited in Islam* (Beirut: The Holy Koran Publishing House, 1984), pp. 326-332.

14. Hammaduh Abdalati, op. cit., p.146.

15. Fazlur Rahman, op. cit, p. 63.

16. Cyril Glassé, op. cit, p. 34.

17. Ibid., p. 186.

18. Eric Davis, *The Christian Century*, January 28, 1987, p. 86.

19. Annemarie Schimmel, *Mystical Dimensions of Islam*, (Chapel Hill: University of North Carolina Press, 1975), pp. 9, 27.

20. Ibid., p. 271.

21. See discussion in Qaradawi, op. cit, pp. 205-207.

22. Jane Smith, "Woman in Islam: Equity, Equality, and the Search for the Natural Order," *Journal of the American Academy of Religion,* XLVII/4, December 1979, pp. 529-530; used by permission.

23. Ibid., p. 530.

24. John J. Donohue and John L. Esposito, eds., *Islam in Transition: Muslim Perspectives,* (New York: Oxford University Press, 1982) in chapter "Social Justice in Islam" by Sayyid Qutb, p. 123.

25. Richard C. Martin, *Islam* (Englewood Cliffs, NJ: Prentice-Hall Inc., 1982), p. 72.

26. National Committee to Honor the Fourteenth Centennial of Islam, 1982, p. 48.

27. Annemarie Schimmel, op. cit., pp. 320-321.

28. Cyril Glassé, op. cit., p. 338.

29. Sulayman S. Mufassir, *Biblical Studies from a Muslim Perspective* (Washington, D.C., The Islamic Center, 1973), p. 14.

30 Geoffrey Parrinder, *Jesus in the Quran* (New York: Oxford University Press, 1977), pp. 110-114.

31. Hammudah Abdalati, op. cit, pp. 160-162.

32. Muslim-Christian Research Group, *The Challenge of the the Scriptures: The Bible and the Quran* (Maryknoll, New York: Orbis Books, 1989), p. 82.

33. Sulayman S. Mufassir, op. cit, p. 14.

34. Alfred Guillaume, *Islam*, (Baltimore: Penguin Books, 1975), pp. 194-199.

35. Ismail al-Faruqi, "Islam and Christianity: Diatribe or Dialogue," *Journal of Ecumenical Studies,* Vol. 3, No. 1, Winter, 1968, p. 58.

36. Leonard Swidler, *Journal of Ecumenical Studies,* September 1984; used by permission. To some of Swidler's observations, I have added my own commentary.

37. Thomas R. Hurst, "Meeting Mufti in the Mosque: An American Experiment in Christian-Muslim Dialogue," *St. Mary's Seminary and University (Baltimore) Alumni Bulletin,* Winter 1991, Vol. 21, No. 2, pg. 11.

38. Frithjof Schuon, *Understanding Islam* (Baltimore: Penguin Books, 1972), p. 16.

39. W. Montgomery Watt, *The Faith and Practice of al-Ghazali* (Chicago: Kazi Publications, 1982), p. 21. Also see Muhammad Haykal, op. cit, p. 215.

Suggested Bibliography

There is a burgeoning bibliography on the culture and religion of Islam. I found the following works most helpful and recommend them for those interested in Christian-Muslim Relations:

Quran

Ali, Abdullah Yusuf. *The Holy Qur'an: Text, Translation, and Commentary.* Printed in the United States by McGregor and Werner, Inc., 1946.

Arberry, Arthur J., Translator. *The Koran Interpreted.* New York: MacMillan Publishing Company, 1976.

Pickthall, M. Marmaduke, Translator. *The Meaning of the Glorious Koran.* New York: New American Library, 1963.

————

Abdalatil, Hammudah. *Islam in Focus.* Delhi: Crescent Publishing Company, 1988.

Abdul-Rauf, Muhammad. *The Islamic View of Women and the Family.* New York: Robert Speller and Sons, 1977.

Ahmad, Khursshid, ed. *Islam: Its Meaning and Message.* Leicester, England: The Islamic Foundation, 1980.

Al-Faruqi, Isma'il. *Islam.* Niles, Illinois: Argus Publications, 1984.

_____ and Lois L. *A Cultural Atlas of Islam*. New York: MacMillan Publishing Company, 1986.

Azis-us-Samad, Ulfat. *A Comparative Study of Christianity and Islam*. Delhi, India: Noor Publishing Company, 1986.

Assam, Abd-al-Rahman. *The Eternal Message of Muhammad*. London: Quartet Books, 1979.

Bezirgan, Basima and Fernea, Elizabeth, eds. *Middle Eastern Muslim Women Speak*. Austin: University of Texas Press, 1977.

Burkhardt, Titus. *An Introduction to Sufism*. Northamptonshire, England: Aquarian Press, 1991.

Chittick, William C. *The Sufi Path of Love: The Spiritual Teachings of Rumi*. Edison, New Jersey: State University of New York Press, 1990.

Cragg, Kenneth. *The Call of the Minaret*. London: Oxford University Press, 1972.

_____. *The House of Islam*. Belmont, California: Dickenson Publishing Company, 1975.

Denny, Frederick M. *Islam*. San Francisco: Harper and Row Publishers, Inc., 1987.

Donohue, John J. and Esposito, John L., eds. *Islam in Transition: Muslim Perspectives*. New York: Oxford University Press, 1982.

Esposito, John L. *Women in Muslim Family Law*. Syracuse: Syracuse University Press, 1982.

_____, ed. *Voices of Resurgent Islam*. New York: Oxford University Press, 1983.

Glassé, Cyril. *A Concise Encyclopedia of Islam*. San Francisco: Harper and Row Publishers, Inc., 1989.

Guillaume, Alfred. *Islam*. Baltimore: Penguin Books, 1975.

Haddad, Yvonne. *Contemporary Islam and the Challenge of History.* Edison, New Jersey: State University of New York Press, 1981.

_____, ed. *The Muslims of America.* New York: Oxford University Press, 1991.

Haykal, Muhammad Husayn. *The Life of Muhammad.* North American Trust Publications, 1976.

Khalifa, Mohammad. *The Sublime Quran and Orientalism.* Karachi: International Islamic Publishers, 1989.

Kimball, Charles. *Striving Together: A Way Forward in Christian-Muslim Relations.* Maryknoll, New York: Orbis Books, 1991.

Lewis, Bernard. *The Arabs in History.* New York: Harper and Row Publishers, Inc., 1967.

_____, ed. *Islam and the Arab World.* New York: Alfred A. Knopf, Inc., 1976.

Lings, Martin. *A Sufi Saint of the Twentieth Century.* Berkeley: University of California Press, 1973.

Long, David. *The Hajj Today.* Edison, New Jersey: State University of New York Press, 1979.

Martin, Richard C. *Islam*. Englewood Cliffs, New Jersey: Prentice-Hall, Inc., 1982.

Mernissi, Fatima. *Beyond the Veil.* New York: Halsted Press, 1975.

Mir, Mustansir. *Coherence in the Qur'an.* Indianapolis: American Trust Publications, 1986.

Momen, Moojan. *An Introduction to Shi'i Islam.* Oxford: George Ronald, 1985.

Muslim-Christian Research Group. *The Challenge of the Scriptures: The Bible and the Qur'an.* Maryknoll, New York: Orbis Books, 1989.

Nasr, Sayyed Hossein. *Ideals and Realities of Islam.* Boston: Beacon Press, 1972.

_____. *Islamic Life and Thought.* Edison, New Jersey: State University of New York Press, 1981.

Parrinder, Geoffrey. *Jesus in the Quran.* New York: Oxford University Press, 1977.

Qaradawi, Yusuf. *The Lawful and the Prohibited in Islam.* Beirut: The Holy Koran Publishing House, 1984.

Rahman, Fazlur. *Islam.* Chicago: University of Chicago Press, 1979.

_____. *Major Themes of the Qur'an.* Minneapolis: Bibliotheca Islamica, 1989.

Saud, Muhammad. *Islam and Evolution of Science.* Islamabad: Islamic Research Institute, 1988.

Schimmel, Annemarie. *Mystical Dimensions of Islam.* Chapel Hill: University of North Carolina Press, 1975.

Schuon, Frithjof. *Understanding Islam.* Baltimore: Penguin Books, 1972.

Smith, Jane, ed. *Women in Contemporary Muslim Society.* Lewisberg, PA: Bucknell University Press, 1978.

Smith, Margaret. *The Way of the Mystics: The Early Christian Mystics and The Rise of the Sufis.* New York: Oxford University Press, 1978.

Smith, William Cantwell. *Islam in Modern History.* Princeton: Princeton University Press, 1957.

Speight, Marston. *God is One: The Way of Islam.* New York: Friendship Press, 1989.

Steward, Desmond. *Early Islam.* New York: Time-Life Books, 1967.

Swartz, Merlin, ed. *Studies on Islam.* New York: Oxford University Press, 1981.

Watt, W. Montgomery. *The Faith and Practice of Al-Ghazali.* Chicago: Kazi Publications, 1982.

_____. *Muhammad: Prophet and Statesman.* London: Oxford University Press, 1977.

Index

Many Arabic terms are included in the Index. For definitions, see the Glossary beginning on page 271.